BEY OUR LIMITS

FAITH DOES RECEIVE THE IMPOSSIBLE

Gaynor van der Hagen

SOLOMON
KEY PUBLISHING

LONDON, UNITED KINGDOM

Gaynor van der Hagen / Solomon Key Publishing

Ordering Information: solomon-key-publishing@protonmail.com

Quantity sales. Special discounts are available on quantity purchases by corporations, associations, and others. For details, contact the "Special Sales Department" at the address above.

Beyond Our Limits / Gaynor van der Hagen. —First ed.

ISBN 978-0-9930762-6-8

This book is dedicated to Samuel, Deborah, Rebecca, and Joshua, our four wonderful children that God entrusted to us. They had no choice but to come along with us on this adventure. We know that their lives have been positively impacted for their future because of the valuable experiences we gained while living in France.
I invite you to come with me on a personal journey of faith, as my husband and I dared to trust God and obey His Word, stepping out into the unknown, beyond our limits.

Gaynor van der Hagen, Surrey, UK, September 2022

"...and go to the land that I will show you."

GENESIS 12:1 (NLT)

CONTENTS

CHAPTER 1

France Here We Come

"Faith is taking the first step, even when you don't see the whole staircase."
Martin Luther King

AFTER FOUR YEARS of anticipation and preparation, we left the UK on the 4th of May 1996 to follow God's calling to Lyon, France. We had great expectations, hopes and dreams about how God was going to use us there. Come with me on a journey as I share about my life as a missionary in France, my tests and testimonies, tears of joy and pain, miracles of provision and healing. This is where God took my husband Paul and I on an adventure *beyond our limits.*

Why did we choose Lyon specifically and what awaited us there? Before I begin to answer these questions and to share our experiences, I will take you back a few years…

My husband Paul was born in Utrecht, Holland and became a Christian at the age of 18 while studying physiotherapy. Soon after that he decided to go to Bible College in Paris. It was there that he felt God call him to be involved in church work in France. Paul realised that he needed to do more practical training in church planting and evangelism and decided that the UK would be the best training ground for him. He had been there once before, participating in the 1989 March for Jesus, and was really excited to see what was happening in the churches there.

In the summer of 1990, he went to the UK for a four-week training course with a church called Ichthus Christian Fellowship, based in London. While there, God unexpectedly gave him an opportunity to receive further training with Ichthus. He therefore enrolled in a one-year course in church planting, evangelism and leadership and worked with an inner-city congregation in South East London.

After completing the course, he expected to return to Holland, but felt that he should stay in London. Paul found a Christian hostel in Waterloo where he could live and managed to find work to support himself. He joined Ichthus Christian Fellowship and attended monthly prayer meetings run by their intercession group for France.

Now about me…

*"Where we love is home - home that our feet may leave,
but not our hearts." Oliver Wendell Holmes, Sr.*

I was born in Harare, Zimbabwe (Salisbury, Rhodesia) to Christian parents. My dad was born in Bradford, England and my mom, in Harare. When I was 13, I went with my youth club to an event held at the Dutch Reformed church in Harare. It was there that I made the most important decision of my life - I became a Christian. As I grew into my teens, however, my excitement for God faded.

My first car

When I was nearly 20, my car (a Datsun 120Y) was stolen. Datsuns were called Japanese takeaways then; they were one of the most popular cars to get stolen as they were so reliable. I had been the proud owner of it for only four months. I decided to use the money from the insurance to buy an open return ticket (an Apex ticket, as it was called), and flew to England with the aim of exploring Europe, obtaining valuable work experience, and then returning home a few months later. I felt alone and very far away from God then. I didn't really have the desire to travel abroad but decided to do so because everyone my age was doing it. I remember looking back with a sense of sadness at the Harare airport balcony (where people stood to wave their loved ones goodbye), while standing at the top of the stairs leading into the aeroplane, wondering when I would return. I called out quietly into the wind, "God, if You are there, will You show Yourself to me when I arrive in England?"

Salisbury Airport

I arrived in London in August 1990 when I was just 20 years old. I moved into a room which I shared with my sister in a Christian hostel in Waterloo. I applied for several jobs and was offered a permanent position as a receptionist, which I accepted because I thought it would enable me to travel around Europe. I found it very difficult to adjust to the pace of life in London, and to be honest, hated it. It was noisy, and there were so many unfriendly looking people dashing everywhere, and I disliked all the grimy looking buildings. I was often sick and had migraines regularly; I think it was the shock of being away from home. Having the Apex ticket meant that I could return home at any time within a three-month period. I realised that if I returned immediately, I would not have achieved my goals to visit certain countries in Europe. With a lot of courage, I tore up my ticket so that I would not be able to return to Zimbabwe immediately and would have to work to save and buy another ticket.

My sister decided to organise a Christmas concert at the hostel and asked for volunteers to sign up to sing in the choir. Paul, who was also staying in the hostel (The Christian Alliance Centre), volunteered to sing in the choir and we met at the rehearsal. He was tall, slim and handsome with blue eyes and a strong Dutch accent and had a surname that I initially found difficult to remember. We seemed to have quite a lot in common. We were Christians, our parents were worried about us, and we were living in a country that wasn't our own. Paul soon realised that I could cook better than him, and so most evenings he would come into the girls' kitchen on the first floor so that I could cook for him. Before Paul and I started dating, he very clearly shared with me a specific calling he had on his life to go to France. He said that if I didn't feel I could go to live in France, he wouldn't date me. His reason was that he did not want to fall in love with someone who would stop him from doing what he believed he was called to do. It seemed like he was proposing to me on the first day, and I found it overwhelming! As you can imagine, I didn't know Paul at all by that stage, and had no desire to go to France. I certainly didn't want to lose my Zimbabwean nationality - of which I was very proud. Nevertheless, I wasn't going to tell him how I honestly felt. I simply told him that I thought it would be great to go to France. In the back of my mind I thought, "If I fall in love with you, then I'll take you back to Zimbabwe with me."

Not long after that, Paul invited me to go to his church. It was different to what I was used to. There were people from all sorts of backgrounds and nationalities - businessmen, people on low income, a lady who was a former prostitute, some with disabilities, musicians and doctors. It was wonderful to see that they all enjoyed being part of the same church. To test me, and on our first date, Paul invited me to help him distribute food to the homeless in a coffee bar based in the "Red Light" district in Soho, London. This was so that he could find out how I would cope working as a missionary in difficult circumstances. It was a very unpleasant environment to be in.

Every Friday evening on our way there, we would have to walk through a dimly lit alley with women standing in their doorways on either side trying to coax men in. One woman took hold of Paul's arm, trying to lure him in when I was holding onto his arm for safety! After quite a long walk, we would arrive at the coffee bar where we would gladly unlock the door and let ourselves in. We met all sorts of homeless people coming in for a free meal - some were alcoholics, drug addicts, punks, prostitutes, both male and female. They would come to get away from their dangerous surroundings and have a safe haven for a few hours while enjoying a hot meal. Others would come to provoke and start a fight. We had to be careful to search every person before they entered the room as we didn't want them to bring in any drugs or alcohol. I would be teamed up with the women, and we would sit and talk to them about God and their lives. It was very satisfying knowing that in some small way, we were helping these people.

One evening, someone managed to get into the coffee bar with a bottle of whisky hidden in the hem of his long shabby coat. Another man tried to follow him in with his bottle of alcohol, but we found it and stopped him entering. He started shouting abusive things across us at the man who had concealed his drink, and almost immediately, ceramic dinner plates started flying through the air as they all joined in the fight. I was hiding under the kitchen table for fear of being hit by one of the plates, and Paul had to shove someone out of the room holding a chair against him to avoid being stabbed with a screwdriver! We locked everyone out who was causing trouble and had to call the police. Unfortunately, not long after that incident, the coffee bar was closed down for health and safety reasons, as there was a requirement to have a corridor between the area where the people ate and the public toilet. That was very sad.

After several months of dating Paul, he could see that I wasn't serious about going to France, and that my family and my country were more important to me. He gave me the weekend to think things over and to pray, but he was seriously considering ending our relationship. I remember crying out to God once again to help me. I picked up my Bible and opened it, desperately hoping something would jump out from the pages at me. My eyes fell across these verses:

So Jesus answered and said, "Assuredly, I say to you, there is no one who has left house or brothers or sisters or father or mother or wife or children or lands, for My sake and the gospel's, who shall not receive a hundredfold now in this time—houses and brothers and sisters and mothers and children and lands, with persecutions—and in the age to come, eternal life."
Mark 10:29-30 (NKJV)

I did not feel that God was telling me I had to go to France, but I believed He was giving me a choice. I believed that as I had previously prayed for a Christian husband, Paul was my answer to prayer, and I did not want to lose him. I also knew that through the Bible verses that I had read, God was telling me that He would bless me. It would not be as I had previously hoped, (having my parents - our future children's grandparents living nearby), but God would give us Christian friends and we would be part of a bigger family, a Church family in France.

In December 1992, a year after we had met, I went to Holland with Paul to meet his family for the first time (yes, we were in separate rooms 😊). His dad was ill in hospital and had asked the hospital staff to move him into a private ward for the day so that he could meet me. He made a big poster that read, "Welcome to Holland," and asked the nurse to put it up at the entrance of the door. He told me that he was so happy to meet his final daughter-in-law (as all of Paul's siblings were already married). I hadn't quite decided at that point to marry Paul but felt honoured that his dad had accepted me. Paul proposed to me shortly after that trip on the banks of the river Thames. I said "Yes" of course, and he phoned my dad in Zimbabwe from Waterloo Station in London to ask for my hand in marriage. My dad gave his blessing, and we began to plan our wedding, which was to be held in Harare, Zimbabwe. After all the details had been decided, the last part to organise was buying the tickets to fly to Zimbabwe for all of us. Sadly, after having bought the tickets for Paul's parents to fly with us, the cancer had rapidly spread to his dad's liver, and he died seven weeks before our wedding. Paul and I then flew to Holland for the funeral, and some people asked us if we should postpone the wedding, but we decided that it was the right thing to go ahead. Paul's Aunt flew over from Canada to accompany his mother on the flight to

Zimbabwe so that she would not be on her own during the wedding. It was very tough.

...And The Two Shall Become One Flesh

"A great marriage is not when the 'perfect couple' comes together. It is when an imperfect couple learns to enjoy their differences." Dave Meurer

In May 1993, one and a half years after first meeting Paul, we were married in Harare at the Trinity Methodist Church - the same church where my parents married. Paul joked that it was a conditional marriage, as it was a condition for us to get married in my home country. 😊

We had our honeymoon in Nyanga and returned to England shortly after that. We began preparing for our future in France and I felt very overwhelmed at times, realising that I had to learn to adjust to yet another culture and to learn a new language as well. At my secondary school (Queen Elizabeth High School in Harare), I was given the choice of learning either Afrikaans or French. As I "knew" I would never live in France, I chose to learn Afrikaans as the easiest option. Funny how we think we know everything when we are young! Afrikaans thankfully wasn't a complete waste of time, as it helped me understand a bit of Dutch. A verse in the Bible that comforted me was given to me by someone at our French prayer group in London: *"Have I not commanded you? Be strong and of good courage; do not be afraid, nor be dismayed for the Lord your God is with you wherever you go." Joshua 1:9 (NKJV)*

I went to French classes in London for a short time but found it very difficult to learn anything. To be honest, I wasn't very motivated at the time and thought that it would be a lot easier to learn French once I was there. We did, however, go on several trips to France to "spy out" the land before eventually moving there. Each time we went we had challenges with transport or health; our trips were never without complications. For three years we tried to leave the UK to make France our home, but didn't see any doors open until...

The Argentinean Connection

*"Continue to remember those in prison as if you were together
with them in prison, and those who are mistreated as if you
yourselves were suffering."*
—Hebrews 13:3 (NIV)

You might wonder how Argentina fits in with France,
but it will soon become clear. On a few occasions in
our church in London we heard Ed Silvoso (an
Argentine evangelist), speak about the revival that was
taking place in his home country. Many years ago, the
Church there used to be divided, weak and very small.
Since the start of the revival there, it has grown
enormously, and many people have become Christians.
It now accounts for over 10% of the population, a
growth of more than 500%.

It excited us to hear about this because we could see
similarities between France today and Argentina before
the revival. In September 1995, two years after we were
married, we attended a conference in Buenos Aires to
experience the revival that impacted this nation. It was
a lovely surprise to meet a pastor from Manchester,
England, that we had previously met at our church
conferences in London, and to get to know her better.

One of our highlights was going to a church that
had ten services a day, seven days a week! The earliest
service started at 7 a.m. and the last was at 11 p.m.
Some 15-20,000 people attended the services each day,
while on Sundays, the whole church gathered in a

football stadium because there was no other place in the capital big enough for them to meet altogether.

While we were in Argentina, we were given the choice of either going to see the Iguazu Falls or to visit Los Olmos, Argentina's biggest maximum-security prison that houses 3,000 criminals, mostly locked up for serious crimes such as murder, rape, robbery etc. It was an obvious choice for us - we wanted to go to the prison and here's why...

A few years before our trip to Argentina, the prison had been in total chaos. Crime was rampant - riots, murders, sexual abuse, extortion and male prostitution were commonplace. The prison was so out of control that the authorities turned the daily running of the prison over to the mafia and the drug dealers that were serving time there. Imagine what this place became when the worst inmates were given the run of it! A Church of Satan was established on the premises and animal sacrifices were offered regularly. Olmos, as the prison is commonly known, was so impregnable, that pastors from the nearby towns had great difficulty getting inside its perimeter. Some inmates reported being tormented by demons who, according to reports, physically materialised in their cells. However, God overturned Satan's plans, and one by one, God started transforming the lives of the prisoners. By the end of 1995, about 45 percent of the prison population had put their faith in Christ and became members of the prison church that had been established.

On our arrival at the prison gates, the ladies were taken into the prison first. We walked through a dark corridor where one prison officer sat behind a desk and collected our passports. Finally, the men were brought in. It was disconcerting to say the least not being able to go in with Paul, and I did not like the idea of leaving my passport either! We were led into a hall where the prisoners were brought in for their church service. The pastor welcomed us and then the praise and worship began. With just one guitar, hundreds of prisoners sang and praised God. It was the most incredible experience I have ever had. The prisoners were singing to God with all the energy they could possibly exude, clapping their hands with all their might and dancing and smiling. Their joy was tangible. It is difficult to truly explain how wonderful it was to experience this, and to see that because their lives had been transformed by the power and love of God, they could be filled with such immense joy despite being in prison for life! I said to Paul afterwards that I sensed it was me who was in prison, because I had never worshipped God in such a free way before. It was such a new and life-changing experience. Seeing how God had transformed the lives of these prisoners was incomparable with going to see any one of The New 7 Wonders of the World!

Los Olmos Prison - Argentina

Why Lyon?

*"When I pray, coincidences happen,
and when I don't, they don't."*
William Temple

During our visit to Argentina, we 'happened' to meet a man who was very interested to hear about our vision for France. He talked to us about a missionary couple (who I'll call Duncan and Betty) that were living in London and planned to start a church in Lyon, France. As soon as we returned to the UK, we arranged to meet them to discuss the possibilities of working with them. They left shortly after that.

At the beginning of 1996, a few months after their arrival in Lyon, we decided to visit them to get to know them better and to visit the city. Three out of the four days that we were with them, we were very ill with gastroenteritis and were not able to do anything that we had planned to do (finding out about the possibilities of accommodation and employment). We had so much opposition that we concluded that this was the place God was calling us to. This was not the only thing that convinced us of course; we had also spent time praying with our leaders in London. Nevertheless, we believed that God had confirmed to us that this was where we were meant to go. Finally, Paul gave up his job working at a translation agency, and I resigned from my position, which by then, was working at Andersen Consulting as a Personal Assistant. Colleagues at our workplaces encouraged us about our imminent departure, and some seemed even envious that we had the determination to leave our comfort zone and start anew.

CHAPTER 2

"Go."
"Here We Go!"

*"Do not lose heart, even if you should
discover that you lack qualities necessary
for the work to which you are called. He
who called you will not desert you, but the
moment you are in need He will stretch
out His saving hand."*
Saint Angela Merici

I BELIEVE GOD had finally opened the doors for us
to go to France. We had three years' experience leading
a home Bible study group, and one year leading the
French prayer group in our church in London. I was
finally ready in my heart, but knew it was impossible to
be fully prepared for the unknown. I had told God that
I was ready to go. However, one night (just weeks

before leaving) half-awake and feeling overwhelmed and fearful, I suddenly heard a very loud voice that shook the whole room. The voice said, "Do not be dismayed for I am with you." Paul was asleep, but not for long, as I shook him and asked him if he had heard the voice. To my surprise, he hadn't heard anything!

The following morning, I opened the Oxford dictionary to look up all the possible meanings of the word "dismayed". This is what I found: "Alarm, Shock, Surprise, Consternation, Concern, Perturbation, Disquiet, Disquietude, Discomposure, Distress, Upset, Anxiety, Trepidation, Fear". Wow, I couldn't believe it, but these were all the emotions that I had been experiencing. God was telling me, however, that it was going to be OK.

A few weeks later, all our belongings, just 40 boxes, were packed and taped up ready to go into the Europcar rental van we had hired. We stopped the van in front of our apartment to load up the boxes. I stood behind the van to take a photo, and to my amazement, I noticed the last two letters on the licence plate - you guessed it, "GO"!! After having said goodbye to our friends and family on Saturday 4 May 1996, we left London behind us and drove to Dover to board our ferry.

As the ferry left, I stood next to Paul on the deck, looking back at the white cliffs of Dover to say our last farewells to England, before heading off to France. Our big adventure had begun. I remember telling him how glad I was to leave England and that I never wanted to return. Little did I know that God would call us back to the UK in December 2012, after 16,5 years of ministry, but that is a story for another book.

Packing our removal van before leaving for France

We crossed the Channel and drove to Holland. The following Monday we began the long eight-hour drive to Lyon. Our friend Richard came with us so that he could drive the rental van back to London. We first stopped over in Holland to say goodbye to Paul's family and to fetch some furniture they were giving us. We left the following day and drove a while before we stopped for a break at a service station, but only to stretch our legs. As we were all sharing driving, we had forgotten to watch the fuel level. We had just left the service station exit when suddenly, as it was my turn to take over, I noticed the fuel level was below a quarter. There was no way to turn back; we just had to keep going and prayed all the way, asking God to make the diesel last long enough to get us to the next one. The wind was blowing against us, and this used our diesel up a lot faster. Our van stopped about 1,5 kilometres from the next fuel station. We discovered what the distance was afterwards, as we couldn't see the fuel station from where we had broken down (and we didn't have smartphones back then 😊).

As you might be aware, it is not a good idea for diesel vehicles to run out of fuel as it can damage the engine. Richard kindly offered to walk the distance to try to buy some fuel. When he arrived, he found out that there weren't any plastic jerry cans for sale to fill up with diesel, so he found one in the bin and used that instead! We prayed before pouring it in and were so thankful that the engine started up immediately. With a bit of initial jumping, we were able to continue our journey and stopped to fill the van up when we arrived at the service station.

Our Arrival In France

"Arriving at one goal, is the starting point to another."
John Dewey

We arrived in Lyon five months after our first visit there. We initially stayed with Duncan and Betty and slept in their living room. Our plan was that I would concentrate on learning French, and Paul would look for a job similar to the one he had in London (desktop publishing). We believed that one day we would be working full-time in Christian ministry but thought that to be established in France, it would be necessary for Paul to find a nine-to-five job. We could then support ourselves financially as we did not want to be dependent on donations and financial support from friends and family.

In our church in London, I had been involved in the worship team and had played the violin in the All Souls Orchestra for many years. I really hoped that I would be able to continue using my musical talents by leading worship in churches in France.

An Open Door?

"You know, God will give favor to anyone who will believe Him. Every day you should confess that you have favor everywhere you go. God will begin to open doors that you wouldn't believe." Joyce Meyer

Several times before we left London, God spoke to us through different people saying, "He had set an open door before us." We didn't experience that when we initially arrived in Lyon. It seemed like everything we tried was unsuccessful, and even something as simple as opening a bank account proved to be complicated.

When we enquired about renting an apartment, we hit another brick wall. We were told that as we did not have work or any other form of income, it would be impossible for us to rent. A letter from a friend in London encouraged us with this Bible verse, which she believed was relevant for our situation:

"I will go before you and make the crooked places straight; I will break in pieces the gates of bronze and cut the bars of iron." Isaiah 45:2 (NKJV)

I will explain later why this was significant. We stayed with Duncan and Betty for six weeks and had a good relationship with them and their two daughters. They helped us in many ways, and we felt very privileged to work with them. They opened their home to us, a two-bedroom apartment, and even stored all our belongings in one part of their lounge - so accommodating of them! One day we were preparing to take Communion in their apartment, and I offered to open a bottle of wine. As I pulled the cork out, it snapped in two and the remaining part of the cork was too short and too far down to be able to use the bottle opener again. I thought of a great idea - well it seemed to be at the time! I found a knife with a blunt blade and pushed it down onto the broken cork to push it into the bottle. It wouldn't budge, so I pushed this time as hard as possible and to my horror, a huge spurt of red wine shot up in the air and hit the ceiling with such force, that it left the ceiling badly stained and it had to be repainted later. Duncan and Betty were very forgiving, but I felt terrible for a long time!

After having stayed with them for a while, we felt it was time to try to find our own accommodation. We plucked up the courage and contacted an estate agent, who showed us an apartment that we thought would be perfect for us. The agent asked Paul if he had work. Paul's answer of course was that he didn't. He then said, "Well, I doubt you will be approved as tenants then, but it's not me who will make the decision - you can try anyway." We produced all the paperwork needed to apply for the tenancy. Usually, if you don't have work, you need to have a guarantor. We decided to play it safe and get two guarantors! We produced the paperwork, but our guarantors did not particularly impress the agency - the first being a missionary (Duncan), and the second, a self-employed tiler originally from the UK, but now living in Lyon. Imagine the expression on the agent's face when they learnt that neither of the guarantors were French! We left the relevant documents with them and felt discouraged; it just didn't seem possible to rent our own place. As we were walking back to Duncan and Betty's apartment, I prayed, "Lord, forgive me for doubting." "If it is Your will for us to get this apartment You can do anything!" It took ten minutes for us to walk back. As Paul unlocked the door, the telephone was ringing. He ran to get it, and it was the Estate Agent telling us that our papers had been accepted, and we could rent the apartment if we paid a deposit by the end of the week. Imagine our excitement! We would finally be able to move into a place we could call home!

A Home Of Our Own

"Love begins by taking care of the closest ones - the ones at home." Mother Teresa

After we had signed all the papers, and had been given the keys, we thought we would finally be able to move our belongings across to our new apartment. We stood at the door and unlocked the top lock. Unlocking the bottom lock was fruitless; it was jammed. Desperate to finally move into our own place, we were extremely frustrated as we still couldn't get in. We had to call a locksmith who drilled a hole through the lock. I then remembered the letter that came from a friend encouraging us with the Bible verse from Isaiah.

"I will go before you and make the crooked places straight; I will break in pieces the gates of bronze and cut the bars of iron." Isaiah 45:2 (NKJV)

This verse meant that we would have challenges, but God would help us to get through each one. Our apartment had been completely painted and redecorated before we moved in and was exactly what we had prayed for. It had two bedrooms, gas central heating, double-glazing and the rent was very reasonable. It was conveniently situated, just a two-minute walk from Duncan and Betty's home, and a ten-minute walk from Lyon's main railway station, Part Dieu. Next door to our apartment was a doctor's practice. We became quite friendly with one of the secretaries there called Marie-Therese, who helped us on several occasions.

Once settled into our apartment, we started to focus on finding employment. We had three months' savings and thought that would be plenty to start us off, giving us time to find temporary work. From having worked in London, our experience was that if you were prepared to do any manual work, for example, washing up, you could find employment rapidly, even if it didn't pay well. However, in Lyon it was a different story. Paul registered with over 30 employment agencies but wasn't offered any work from any of them. As his name was one of the last to be put on their registers, the first person to be offered work was the one who had been registered the longest. Another huge challenge was that we needed to have a residence permit ("carte de séjour") to be employed and to be allowed to stay in France.

By August 1996, three months after our arrival, Paul still hadn't been able to find any form of employment, and many companies had closed for the holidays. Finding work was almost impossible at that time of year, as many companies slowed down for the summer holidays. Although our money was running low, we believed that God wanted us to return to the UK to attend our church's summer retreat called "Revival Camp". We felt we could get some rest, pray with others and think clearly about how to move forward. We were obliged to return to the UK at that time anyway, as the ruling was that if you had no employment after three months of living there, you were obliged to return to your home country to have your passport stamped. Once stamped, we were able to return for a further three-month period to look for work.

While in the UK, we met an English missionary working in Burkina Faso, West Africa. He prayed for us and felt that God had told him to give us £500 to pay for me to attend a language course. We had never met him before, but God used him in a wonderful way. I believe that from his own experiences as a missionary and learning to trust God by faith, it led him to have compassion on us. His obedience to God and generous gift opened several doors for us.

On our return to Lyon, we had another big challenge to overcome before I could enrol in the nine-month language course with "Alliance Française". To be able to apply for a student visa, we needed to have 50,000 French Francs in our bank account (approximately £5,000), showing that we were able to support ourselves for the duration of the course. The problem was that we had already used up our savings on living expenses over a three-month period, as we had not been able to find work. We were really stuck and knew that without that sum of money, we would have to return to England, but we didn't have enough money to return! A friend of ours had a brilliant idea -

he would lend us the money for one day. The Visa Bureau only needed to have proof that the money was in our account, and then I could go ahead and register with the language school. He transferred the money into our account; we printed out a bank statement and took it to the Visa Bureau and they approved our application. He then withdrew his money the following day. We knew that even though we didn't have the money that they thought we would need to support ourselves for the year, we had God.

"Now to Him who is able to do exceedingly abundantly above all that we ask or think, according to the power that works in us." Ephesians 3:20 (NKJV)

Dealing With French Bureaucracy

I would like to explain a little of what we were up against in this wonderful country. Most foreigners have an 'epic' tale to tell of their dealings with it. One should be prepared for a lot of frustration caused by time-wasting officials. Often you may wonder whether the right hand knows what any other part of the body is up to (it usually doesn't) and one must expect to receive conflicting information from consulates, government departments, "prefectures" and town halls. Red tape is a way of life in France, where every fourth worker is a civil servant. To obtain any sort of permit, you must complete numerous forms, answer dozens of irrelevant questions and provide mountains of documents with official translations to produce an impressive-looking dossier.

To be able to study in France, I needed to get a student residency permit, and to be able to obtain that, I needed to be covered by the French health insurance, known as the "Assurance Maladie" (A.M.). As we had already been out of the UK for three months, the British National Health Service (NHS) no longer covered us, and as we hadn't worked in France, we couldn't get health cover. A lady at the A.M. helpdesk asked me what would happen if I was to get sick without cover. I told her, "Well, I'll get sick!" I knew that if I talked to her about God looking after me, she would think I was completely loony! She didn't like my response and told me that she would do me a special favour. She organised a student health cover for the period of my course, which initially was for nine months. The cost was just £90 for nine months, just £10 a month, which I might add, for us at that time was a lot as we didn't have much.

My course began in October 1996. One week later, I missed having my period and after buying a tester from the pharmacy, discovered I was pregnant. My health cover was to expire at the end of June 1997, and our first baby was born mid-June 1997. All hospital bills, ultrasound scans and blood tests were covered by the medical insurance. Obtaining my new student social security number enabled me to get the relevant health cover that I needed. God is so good! I went to our local doctor to register my pregnancy. I expected him to say "congratulations," but was utterly shocked to hear what came out of his mouth. He asked me if I wanted to have the baby aborted! I couldn't believe it. He continued, "Well, I didn't know if you were happy to be pregnant, and that is why I asked if you would like the option to abort the baby." It shocked me to think that doctors would even ask that question! I then realised that for some women who perhaps hadn't planned a pregnancy, being offered the option to abort could push them over the edge to make a hurried decision that one day they would later live to regret.

We announced our good news to family and friends, and it was very interesting to see the variety of reactions we received. Some asked how many months pregnant I was. As it was just a few weeks, they thought it probably wasn't a wise idea to be sharing the news just yet, just in case something went wrong, and I had a miscarriage. I decided that if God had given me a child, He was going to protect it and that there was no need to let fear rule my life. I gave no room for a possibility of a miscarriage. I was determined that from then on, each pregnancy would be announced immediately, and I would not give in to any negative talk or allow it to be spoken over me and my pregnancy. Another person told me that I was crazy to fall pregnant when Paul didn't have work and asked me how I was going to afford to buy everything I needed for our baby. Believe it or not, after just four months into the pregnancy, Christians from a nearby church had given us more than we ever needed. Paul's mom, sister and brother-in-law also brought us some baby furniture from Holland, and Paul's sister gave me an intensive course on how to fold Terry Towelling nappies. Thankfully I didn't have to use them! God had provided for all our needs.

As my student fees had been paid for, my student status enabled us to apply for a residency permit. This was finally granted after six months of several unsuccessful attempts. As Paul and I were married, he was granted a normal residency permit which enabled him to start looking for work. The doors had been opened because of one faithful missionary who chose to obey God's prompting. We no longer had to leave the country every three months. Phew!

"If you talk to a man in a language he understands, that goes to his head. If you talk to him in his language, that goes to his heart." Nelson Mandela

I knew I had to learn French to be able to communicate effectively, so I attended an intensive language course with the "Alliance Française" three hours a day, five days a week. Just pregnant, I found it very challenging with morning sickness a regular occurrence. It was difficult to learn as well, not only because languages didn't seem to be my forte, but also because I was surrounded by young people who were there just for the fun of it. Often the girls in my class would lay their hands on my bump to see if they could feel the baby moving inside me. How was I ever going to concentrate with them around me? I also wondered how I would ever understand any French. My French teacher, Didier, would walk into the class and immediately start waffling away in French. Not understanding a thing, apart from the usual "bonjour," I thought he was crazy! What was he going on about?

As we were struggling financially, I had noticed a small advert on the noticeboard at the language school. Someone was looking for an English student to teach English to two young French children. I scribbled the phone number down and discussed it with Paul when I went home. I decided to call. The gentleman who had placed the advert was a dentist and wanted me to go to his home to speak to his children for two hours once a week. He offered to pay 60 francs which was the equivalent of £6. I couldn't believe how little he was paying, but when you need the money… I arranged to go to the house. The bus journey was long, probably about 45 minutes to get there, and the bus fare cost me half of what I was being paid! I was met by the gentleman who called his children into the lounge to meet me. I think they were too young to sit down for five minutes, let alone for two hours!

Anyway, I went to their bedroom and found some English books they had on the shelf. I found a book with animal pictures in it and thought it would be a good one to start with. I tried to encourage the children to sit on the floor so that I could get their attention, but as soon as I started reading English words out, they started jumping up and down and shouting the words out loud. Then, almost as if stung by a bee, they started running around the room and then flung themselves onto the bed doing somersaults.

Finally, after about half an hour of expelling their energy, I managed to get them to sit quietly for a few minutes. "Horse, say after me, horse," I said. The little boy jumped up quickly from the floor and said, "Non, non!" "Papa dit 'orse, donc c'est 'orse!!!" ("Daddy says 'orse, so it is 'orse!"). I went to their house at least three times but taking into consideration the time it took for me to get there and the little pay I received, I decided that it was not worth going anymore.

One morning in my class at the "Alliance Française", Didier told us that we were going to learn how to count in French. He explained for three hours how to say the numbers in French. I hadn't a clue what he was talking about. Why was 70 said, 60 + 10, and 80, 4 x 20, and as for 90, 4 x 20 + 10? I was completely lost. Believe it or not, I had only one day to grasp this (which I didn't) before moving on to another topic. We told jokes amongst ourselves and chatted in English. The not-so-fun part though, was the homework that I had to do each afternoon. Not having understood anything, I had to try and decipher it at home, and what should normally have taken one hour to complete, used to take me longer to do in the afternoon than the actual course in the morning!

My teacher told us that to improve our French pronunciation, we were to read any text that we saw out loud to ourselves whenever we were out and about. He said it would help us to gain confidence as well.

One day, I remember sitting in the car while Paul was driving; I was reading out loud billboards and graffiti along the way. Suddenly I said something in French and Paul was completely shocked. He told me never to repeat what I had said again, as it was a swear word. It was quite funny really as I hadn't a clue what I was reading out, it was just a load of words to me.

People suggested that it would be a good idea for Paul to talk only to me in French at home, but that was just too much for me and I landed up crying - a lot!! My best friend, my husband, was the only one I felt I could share everything with and trying to converse in French with him was not a good thing for our relationship at all, and so unnatural. We gave up on that idea and I just continued to plod along on my own. It was hard work in my French lessons, but I eventually started enjoying it and made some good friends there.

One of my friends from college, an American girl called Laurel, didn't turn up in class after the weekend. We all wondered where she was. Then Didier came into the classroom looking very sombre. He produced an article from the newspaper which talked about a girl by the name of Laurel who had been raped, beaten up and left for dead. I tried to phone her mobile phone, but there was no reply. We realised that it had to be her. We told the hospital that we were pastors and took the opportunity to go and pray with her while she was in intensive care. She was so grateful. We had to inform her family, and they came from the States to visit her. She recovered slowly but returned to her home with her parents soon after that. After a few months of learning French, we started learning how to debate in French, and surprisingly, or maybe not, the first topic was on abortion! To sit and hear that half the class was 'for' abortion turned my stomach! I could feel our beautiful child moving inside me, and it upset me so much. After almost five months of intense French lessons, I finally decided that I was too tired to continue doing it full-time and stopped going.

Our Hopes For France

Believing God had called us to live and work in France, we wanted to invest our lives there and see many new churches established. We also wanted to see existing churches working together in unity, reaching the nation of France with the Gospel. Many people believe that revival, similar to that in South America, would start in the UK and then affect the rest of Europe, including France.

France plays a central role in Europe politically, as well as economically. A revival in France would not only affect Europe, but also the rest of the world, as some 500 million people in 50 different countries speak French. Since the 17th century, when the Protestant church accounted for 50% of the French population, France has not seen any significant spiritual renewal. Lyon is France's second largest city (those living in Marseille would disagree) with over 1,2 million inhabitants and it is a hub of financial and cultural activity. It is also famous for being France's gastronomic capital. Perhaps this was why we often had friends joking with us about our real motivations for going to live in France – cheese and wine? ☺ Unfortunately, it was also claimed that Lyon was the occult capital of Europe, which meant more people would regularly go to visit a 'faith healer' than visit a GP.

Getting Ourselves Established

We believed that God had called us to be "tentmakers" (meaning to look after ourselves financially), but our financial situation and struggle to find employment was a huge challenge. We trusted that God would look after us and therefore decided not to tell anyone (not even our own family) about our financial difficulties. One day we were walking in central Lyon in a neighbourhood called Foch. We didn't have any money left to buy food for that day and we just 'happened' to walk past a Social Services office. We both looked at each other and seemed to have the same thought - perhaps they could help us in our desperate situation. We went in and found a lady sitting at a desk in a room that seemed very bare. She had a pad of paper with a list of names on it and a money box on her desk, and that was about it. We sat down and told her that we were unable to buy food for the week and had no work. She asked us our names and wrote them down. She then proceeded to reach into her box and took out 200 francs (about £20) from an envelope and handed it to us. We couldn't believe it. We didn't have to sign anything or prove anything; we simply took the money and left. God had provided for us for that week, and it was amazing trusting Him!

After nine months of us both looking for work, Paul started a part time job in our neighbourhood delivering Chinese fast food and pizzas on a moped for a couple of hours a day. It was the first job he was offered after moving into our apartment - it wasn't one he had applied for either! The husband of a lady in our church owned a Chinese take-away restaurant and pizzeria and needed a person for home deliveries. It wasn't exactly what we had in mind when we prayed for a job, but it gave Paul an opportunity to practice his French and meet many people. Whizzing around Lyon during the rush hours and late at night on a moped was not a particularly safe way of traveling, but one positive result was that Paul's prayer life increased significantly!! It was an interesting experience to say the least. I had to laugh as Paul's uniform was a pair of bright orange overalls. He would sometimes ride past our apartment, and I would see him as I was looking out of the window, and he would stop and wave.

We saw God provide miraculously through several people, always just in time before our savings ran out. The Bible talks about tithing, giving ten percent of your earnings to God. Each time we were given some money, or Paul earned some money, we gave ten percent to church. It was a difficult thing to do, especially when we did not know where our next income was going to come from. God was teaching us how to live by faith and to trust Him to provide in every situation. However, two months after we moved into our first apartment, I started getting very nervous about our financial situation. Women have a need to feel secure, and I was feeling anything but secure at the time, and probably being pregnant made it much worse! Paul's delivery job was not paying enough to cover our rent, let alone pay for our food and electricity bills. Our rent was 2,500 francs a month, and Paul's salary was 2,200 francs. Even so, we continued to keep quiet about our difficult financial situation as we still believed that God would do miracles for us. Many times, I would walk out of our apartment building and see a beggar sitting there with his bowl begging for money. To tell you the truth, I felt like sitting next to him and begging with my own bowl as I was afraid to completely trust God. My mind was working overtime trying to see how I could solve our problems because of fear. I felt our financial situation was out of control and I thought I would try to take control of it myself. I remembered that initially we had paid a two-month deposit to the letting agency. I thought that I could phone them and explain that we had made a mistake by renting our apartment. I would then tell them that they could keep the deposit and we could then pull out and go back to living with Duncan and Betty.

That Sunday, just before telling Paul what I was thinking about, Duncan preached on a story about

Elijah who was a prophet from the Bible in the Old Testament. Elijah was in the desert and God provided for his needs by placing him near a stream where he could drink and sent him ravens to feed him. (1 Kings 17:10) The story continues that after a time, the river dried up and the ravens ceased coming. God did not immediately speak and tell Elijah what to do. Elijah had to wait for God to give him direction. God finally spoke up and told him that he had to go to Zarephath to meet a widow. Elijah perhaps thought that the widow would provide for his needs. In actual fact, Elijah had to find enough faith for himself, as well as for the widow and her son, in order that they would all survive the terrible famine at that time.

I realised that God was speaking to me through Duncan's message. God had not told us to pack our bags and leave the apartment. We were to wait for Him to tell us what to do. Sometime later that same week, we received an email from a pastor in Manchester, England that we had met when we were in Argentina. She told us that God had spoken to her to send us £500. She asked for our English bank account details and immediately transferred the money to us. It was an amazing experience living by faith, and so exciting to see God provide for us. We would not have had enough to pay for the rent that month had she not listened and obeyed God's voice! We cut out buying snacks and yoghurts and were very careful with our money. I believe that because we had decided to tithe right at the beginning, God honoured that. We always had food on the table and never lacked anything and were happy trusting God. I believe God tested us during these times to see if we really trusted Him. The Bible says in Malachi,

"Bring all the tithes into the storehouse, that there may be food in My house, and try Me now in this," says the Lord of hosts, "If I will not open for you the windows of heaven and pour out for you such blessing that there will not be room enough to receive it." Malachi 3:10 (NKJV)

Also, in the book of Luke, the Bible says:

"He who is faithful in what is least is faithful also in much; and he who is unjust in what is least is unjust also in much." Luke 16:10 (NKJV)

We knew that if we did what was right with only a little, God would in time bless us with more, and we would then have the wisdom to know how to manage more.

Dreaming Again

"Follow your passion, be prepared to work hard and sacrifice, and, above all, don't let anyone limit your dreams." Donovan Bailey

One night, while Paul was still working for the Chinese takeaway restaurant, I had a dream that God was going to give us a house. I saw a house that had an outdoor staircase leading up to the front door. There was a balcony, and an elderly woman was leaning on it with folded arms, looking down at us. Paul thought it was a great dream and we laughed, wondering how it would be possible for us to have our own home as it was a constant struggle to pay the rent each month. Nevertheless, we started to pray that God would, one day, fulfil that dream.

A short while after we moved into our new apartment, we once again had no money to buy food and had nothing to eat for that evening. I had gone out to the local park so that Samuel could play on the slides and rocking horses. I met a lady that I had spoken to a couple of times before, who often took her grandson to the park to play; he was the same age as Samuel. She came up to me and said, "I was thinking of you today, and want to give you this." She put 100 francs (£10) in my hand and said, "Here, this is for Samuel." I asked her why she wanted to give it to me, and she said she just felt like giving it. She also gave me some lovely new clothes which she had bought for her grandson. Her daughter didn't like them, and I couldn't understand why, because they were just fabulous! Samuel did get a part of that money that day, as I used it to buy food and we all shared it together. On another occasion when we had no food, a friend from church popped around with a basket full of fresh produce. One more miracle we had was that someone based in Bristol in England paid some money into our English bank account. We did not know anyone living in Bristol, and still to this day don't know who it was from. We continued to believe that as God had called us, He was faithful and would always provide for everything we needed.

Work And Work Permits

"I learned the value of hard work by working hard."
Margaret Mead

As I mentioned, right from the first day we arrived Paul had been looking for work. Even though he had a Dutch passport and was officially allowed to work in France, there was a lot of paperwork involved in enrolling into the French social security system. The biggest obstacle though, was not having a work permit ("carte de séjour"), which would allow him to work. No one could get a job without this document, neither could they obtain a work permit without a job offer. For this reason, Paul needed to find a permanent position or a temporary job that lasted longer than three months to enable us to stay in the country. He had interviews for two permanent positions working in publishing, but no responses. I am sure that it is surprising for you to read this, as the European laws have changed and when holding a European passport, you can now stay as long as you like in France. Paul tried to find various types of jobs ranging from factory worker, security guard, driver, to selling hamburgers at McDonald's. For some positions they told him he was over-qualified, or, that he did not have the right qualifications. Almost every job required a French diploma or some experience that he did not have. Would you believe that to be a window cleaner you had to have a window-cleaning diploma, and to pick up debris from the motorway, you had to have another special type of diploma? Many jobs would require the baccalaureate qualification, with perhaps two years previous study at university. Each time we saw the word 'baccalaureate', our hearts sank - as although Paul had passed his exams in Holland, they were not recognised in France. We used to joke and say, "Well, the only "bac" we have is a "bac à sable" - which is the French word for sandpit! ☺

September 1996

Paul continued to visit agencies, hoping to find any form of temporary employment. His name was obviously still at the end of the list. It was an extremely frustrating situation to be in - to want so desperately to work and not have the opportunity to prove yourself. I was so proud of Paul though as he never gave up. Paul also looked into the possibility of going on training courses, as any job in France seemed to require a French qualification. He was unsuccessful on many occasions. He also enquired at the Jobcentre to see if he would be eligible for any grants provided for the unemployed but had no reply for a long time.

Racking our brains for ideas, we thought more seriously about starting up a small business or becoming self-employed. Our preliminary inquiries weren't encouraging and confirmed our suspicions - it would be a daunting and very lengthy undertaking. There would have been an enormous amount of paperwork involved, and we were told that start-up loans from banks or government agencies were as rare as penguins in the desert. We were left with little choice but to press on and pray and knock on any door until one opened.

CHAPTER 3

New Beginnings

*"Learn from yesterday, live for
today, hope for tomorrow."
Albert Einstein*

WE DECIDED THAT IT would be a good idea to keep in touch with our family, friends and prayer supporters by sending out newsletters to them regularly. This was the first one that we wrote in January 1997:

> We hope you are warming up as Europe returns to normal again after the extreme, "Siberian" temperatures that hit us over the past month? At the beginning of January, we returned from a very exhausting trip to the Spanish Pyrenees where we visited my brother

who runs a restaurant there. My sister came to visit us from England and drove us there.

I cannot believe that I am already four months pregnant! It was so lovely to get away for a short holiday and to spend some time with my family again. On our return, we were caught in a terrible snowstorm. Our little rental car had no snow tyres or snow chains, and the conditions were treacherous. We prayed all the way back, asking God to protect us and help us to be able to drive through all the snow. It was cold and the snow was falling heavily and quickly settled on the roads. Cars were slipping everywhere, and we were concerned that the motorways would be closed, and that we would have an even more challenging drive home if we couldn't make it onto the motorway.

Our concerns turned into a reality when we saw the police block off the motorway just as we arrived. Many lorries that were stuck in the snow had blocked the motorway and we had to use alternative routes and go down isolated country lanes, where there were no streetlights. For most of the journey, our car was the only one on the road. I was afraid that if we became stuck, we might die in the freezing cold. Amazed that we were still able to drive through the snow in such a small car, we passed several cars that had stopped on the road because they were stuck in the snow. We saw a BMW, equipped with snow tyres, that had slipped off the road into a ditch. The biggest shock was to come across a snow plough that had slipped off the road and was lying on its side!! Instead of eight hours it took us 15 hours to drive home, as there was at least 30 cm of snow on the roads. On our return, we heard that thousands of cars were stranded on the motorway, and people had to spend the night in public buildings and schools. It was reported that some people who had left their cars on the motorways had died that night from the cold as they tried to find help. We were very glad to get back. We knew that God had done yet another miracle by keeping us safe and enabling us to get back so that my sister would not miss her return flight to the UK. We thanked Him for His protection, and we were also grateful for my sister's excellent driving skills.

The Church-plant In Lyon

After a couple of months preparation, our first church meeting started in the new apartment of Pastor Duncan and Betty. The church was a branch of a South American mission, but was also supported by a church in Manchester, UK. We wanted to see the Word of God being proclaimed with signs and wonders, darkness lifted, multitudes saved, and a new generation being raised up by God. Our meetings began with ten adults and six children attending on Sunday mornings (our service was initially in English) - it sounds small, but you have to begin somewhere. The apartment that

Duncan and Betty had purchased a year previously for the meetings was slowly being renovated. We cleared out the shop front on the ground floor in preparation for the meetings. A church in Birmingham gave us an overhead projector, and the next step was to buy 20 chairs.

We met on Thursday nights as a worship team to learn new songs and practice our instruments. Friday nights were spent praying together. On Sunday mornings we met for one hour before the meeting to pray, and once a month we took the Lord's Supper and ate lunch together afterwards. We planned to start monthly prayer evenings with another church in our neighbourhood. Even though it was early days, it was a very important time for us as a new church. An English couple, originally from Aldershot in the UK, had joined our church. to help us. They had three young children and lived just outside Lyon.

A few times during the week we would get together to pray, and our Sunday services drew the attention of neighbours as we often had the windows open; the sound of the violin, guitar and singing was clearly heard by anyone passing in the street, or those living nearby. One neighbour told us that we were the talk of the neighbourhood and said that people wondered if we were Catholics or some religious cult (that was obviously their fear!). Our neighbourhood was very cosmopolitan with people from many different ethnic backgrounds - Algerians, Jews, Armenians, Turkish, Chinese, Portuguese, English and French of course.

The people were very friendly and polite, and we had good relations with the local baker, grocer and the newsagent.

To get around we did a lot of walking and used the public transport; we missed the use of our Peugeot 205 that we used to drive in London. In April that year a team of 40 teenagers visited our church. They were a team of South American missionaries linked to the church in Manchester. They did street evangelism, and their singing and drama attracted many people. Several people wanted to find out more about who we were. Our church also participated in a 40-day prayer and fasting time during Pentecost.

CHAPTER 4

Early Days

*"Communication works for
those who work at it."*
John Powell

NOT ONLY DID WE SEND OUT newsletters, but we also set up a prayer chain - a list of people willing to pray whenever we needed it most. Living in Lyon felt very oppressive, and it often seemed difficult to pray. It was wonderful to know that we had people praying for us around the world if we were struggling with anything. Occasional visits from my parents, siblings and Paul's mom helped too. We welcomed visitors from our church in London as well as friends and other relatives. We reminded them that the baguettes and cheese and wine would be ready waiting for them on arrival 😊. Lyon is such a beautiful city with the Rhone and Saone rivers flowing through it. It is conveniently located, and many visitors would drive through "en route" to somewhere else, popping in to stay overnight with us.

Our fax machine and modem enabled us to send emails and fax prayer requests. It seems funny to even mention this now as technology has evolved so much. Our prayer requests were mainly for success in work, our involvement in starting the new church and adapting to the new culture. We also asked for prayer for our relationships with other missionaries, that we would be fruitful and would be able to learn the language.

Team Relationships

In September 1996, we officially launched our French-speaking church services. We had not publicised our meetings before as we did not have an appropriate meeting place. From then onwards we began to have our church meetings in French, as well as English. We had a successful start having excellent weather for our open-air events, singing in French and English. Many people stopped to listen and chat with some of our team members.

On the first afternoon at one of our public outreach meetings, only half an hour after setting up on the streets with our banners, flags and instruments, we were questioned by police officers who arrived in a patrol car. They wanted to know if we were a "sect" (cult). They only left after we assured them that we were part of an umbrella organisation of local evangelical churches. It was a bit scary. There is a great fear of cults in France, so to be effective it was important to win people's trust. It seemed that the most effective way to make disciples was through personal evangelism, in other words, by making friends. France seemed to be very wary of cults and following a mass suicide of the "Solar Temple" cult in 1995 in the French Alps, the French government commissioned an official investigation into hundreds of different cults. These were mainly New Age cults that were active throughout the country. Many Protestant churches were also incorrectly labelled as cults. For this reason, we needed a lot of wisdom to overcome common misunderstandings when we talked to people about our church. At the same time, it was important not to be intimidated, or fearful of public opinion, but to have a clear Christian testimony.

We were encouraged by the way the church was moving ahead. We had some 30 people (visitors included), attending the service. We still met in Duncan and Betty's front room, but soon would have to move to the 'shop' on the ground floor. We would then be more visible as a church for anyone passing by, and it would make it easier to invite visitors. The following Sunday some 200,000 people took to the streets to watch a carnival in the centre of Lyon. It was an excellent opportunity to be able to talk to people about

God, although it wasn't very easy to compete with the noise of many drums!

Why Grenoble?

As Paul was still looking for work, a Christian accountant we knew who worked in the recruitment department of the SNCF (the French Railways), was a tremendous help looking for opportunities for Paul. He helped Paul get an interview but unfortunately Paul passed only two of the three tests. He was so disappointed and discouraged when he came home that he went to sit in his office to be alone. His office was a cupboard in our corridor where he had managed to assemble a desk and could just about sit on his chair. After a few minutes, he suddenly shouted out to me. He had found a fax that had come in. It had curled up, slipped off the fax machine and rolled onto the floor. It was a job offer for full-time employment in Grenoble! After looking for a job for ten months he was finally able to start work the following week. He began on the 9th of March 1997. Since August/September the previous year (when our savings had run out), money had miraculously been coming in from different people which gave us one month's grace each month!

"Then the manna ceased on the day after they had eaten the produce of the land; and the children of Israel no longer had manna; but they ate the food of the land of Canaan that year."
Joshua 5:12 (NKJV)

This was a verse that we had held onto for those first ten months as we were trying to settle. During that period, our faith was tested and sometimes we felt like giving up. Praise God, He is faithful and He sustained us in many ways. We believed that God had told us He would continue to provide for us, just like He did for the widow in the Bible that had no food left apart from a handful of flour and a little oil in a jar. She and her son were preparing to die. In brief, a miracle happened for them, and they were able to have enough until the end of the drought. We felt that God was saying that money would continue to come in until Paul found a permanent job. We really appreciated the people that had been praying for us. We felt invigorated after this breakthrough.

Paul's employment in Grenoble meant a five-hour commute every day! He would leave very early in the morning and return after 8 pm each night. This was so difficult for me as I did not speak French well enough to converse and felt very alone. I love to talk - like most women, and not being able to communicate made me afraid to leave our apartment in case someone spoke to me. During the first week at his new company, Paul's employer (and boss) announced he was leaving his job and that he would be replaced by a French female manager. Paul could not believe it; the guy who had only just employed him had left! To make matters worse, the new manager did not have any idea why Paul had been employed in the first place and told him that she did not think they would be able to keep him on.

Can you imagine our disappointment?! Paul 'knew' then that his three-month contract would not be renewed.

Thankfully though, God did amazing things again. Paul told his new boss that I was pregnant and begged her to keep him on. After working for three months, she once again threatened to stop his contract. She said that there wasn't anything for him to do but decided to keep him on anyway. She changed his job title and offered him another three-month contract. At the end of that period, she told Paul he would not be staying. Once again, he pleaded with her, and again, so that she could legally keep him on and not have to employ him permanently, he was given a new job title. This time, however, she lowered his salary! She also said that she did not want to offer him a permanent position because she wanted us to move to Grenoble so that Paul would be "more available."

By the grace of God, Paul's contract was renewed twice, and he worked there for a total of nine months before it finally came to an end on the 16th of December 1997. When he went to the Jobcentre to register as unemployed, he found out that obtaining unemployment benefit was only possible if a person had worked a minimum of nine months! Can you believe it? God had been keeping him on for a reason! While he continued to look for another job, he was paid 75% of his previous salary per month, which kept us going. What a miracle!

Winter 1997

*"To learn a language is to have one more window
from which to look at the world."*
Chinese Proverb

Our baby was due on the17th of June and had started
to make its presence known by the occasional kicks
(more often at night!). I was then 19 weeks pregnant,
and my little bump was showing quite nicely. I was well
with my pregnancy and our baby was above average
size for dates - not surprising really with parents as tall
as us. We went for numerous (routine) check-ups and
visited the local hospital sometimes two or three times
a week. My gynaecologist was a very nice Frenchman
who refused to speak one word of English to me - even
though he had done a lot of his studies in English. In
our experience, it seems that the French do not want
to make any mistakes when trying to speak English, so
they would rather not speak it at all. I did not have a
clue what he was saying most of the time and was
grateful that Paul was able to come with me for each
examination. At my first appointment with him, he
asked me where I was born. I told him that my mother
was born in Zimbabwe and my father in England. He
then asked me, "Oh, so is your mother black then?"
He then saw my surprised face and went bright red, as
he realised his mistake when he took another look at
me and realised that I was white.

One of the check-ups that I had at the hospital was very strange. I was taken into a room where there was an Arabic woman who couldn't speak French or English and looked quite old to be pregnant. She had electrodes on her tummy, was being monitored by a machine and was extremely overweight. I was put on the other monitor in the room and was told to lie quietly. I must have been there for over an hour. Paul was not allowed to come in the room with me and neither of us knew why I was being monitored so closely. Thankfully they did not ask me to do another test, so everything must have been OK. The French take antenatal care very seriously. At that stage of pregnancy, I was beginning to feel a little uncomfortable and had trouble sleeping. One specialist thought that the birth would be at the beginning of June, although we still expected it to be roughly two weeks later.

CHAPTER 5

"Speak LORD, I Am Listening"

"Being a mother is not about what you gave up to have a child, but what you've gained from having one."
Sunny Gupta

NO ROOM? Two days after I was due to give birth to our first child, my contractions started at 3 a.m. We went into the hospital mid-morning; I was tired, and we had to stay there for hours without any food. We were eventually told that there was no room for me to give birth there and that I had to be transferred by ambulance to another hospital. Members of staff argued as to who was going to pay for the ambulance to transfer me to another hospital.

Finally, I was taken to the ambulance and Paul was told to follow us in his car. I didn't really understand what was going on as my French was poor then. The labour was long and exhausting. I had hired a TENS machine from England which gives an electric current produced by a device to stimulate the nerves for therapeutic purposes. It was to help me with the labour pains. Unfortunately, it wasn't positioned properly on my back and all it did was leave burn marks!

Our baby's head had just started to come out and the nurse told me I could touch it, which helped to encourage me. When the time came to push, it was really challenging. Unfortunately, his shoulder was stuck, and they had to pull hard to get him out. At 19:05 my reward came. Yes, our baby was a reward from the hard labour. My mother reminded me, "Remember, your baby will be your wonderful reward after your hard labour."

The nurse took him quickly to be weighed, a beautiful boy, healthy and pink with very blond hair, so blond that you could hardly see it. He had a large hematoma on his head - a big kind of bump which we think was there because he had spent time upside down in the womb for a while. We were told it would go away after a couple of weeks. I hadn't even noticed it, as to me, he was just the most beautiful baby in the world!

When he was examined, they discovered he had a fractured collar bone from being pulled out roughly, but as babies' bones are soft at birth, it healed quickly.

The birth announcement read:

The Lord has filled my heart with joy;
how happy I am because of what He has done!
—1 Samuel 2:1 (GNT)

It is with great thankfulness and joy that we announce the birth
of our son Samuel, born June 1997 at 19.05, weighing
4.010kgs, at Hôpital Saint Joseph, Lyon.

"Before I formed you in the womb
I knew you…" — Jeremiah 1:5 (NIV)

All was well and I stayed in the hospital for four days until Samuel regained the weight he had lost. Just a few days after he was born, I was lying in my hospital bed feeding him, when I heard some wonderful music being played just outside my window. It was my first experience of the "Fête de la musique", the annual music festival. Each year in June, France has an all-day musical celebration; roads are closed off and people can make music in the streets. It was as if Samuel and I were given our own private concert, and what an amazing experience it was!

We applied for a Dutch passport for him, as getting a British one was too complicated and costly. We were not able to apply for French citizenship for him because to qualify, one of his parents needed to be

French. At birth he was taller than the national average, and he gained more than one kilogram in just four weeks, which was double the national average!

A Police Summons

> *"The toilets at a local police station have been stolen.*
> *Police say they have nothing to go on."*
> *Ronnie Barker*

In September 1997, Paul received a summons from the police. We thought this might be related to the ongoing police investigations into sects, which the authorities were very much weary of. We had nothing to hide of course, but it still made us feel uncomfortable. We thought it might be an excellent opportunity to share our faith, and as the Bible says, "always be prepared to give an answer to everyone who asks you to give the reason for the hope that you have. But do this with gentleness and respect." 1 Peter 3:15 (NIV). We asked our prayer partners to pray for Paul so that he would be prepared for whatever questions they would ask him. It was funny, as it turned out to be a formality regarding Samuel's birth registration!

CHAPTER 6

Winter 1998

"No winter lasts forever;
no spring skips its turn."
Hal Orland

LYON WAS COVERED in 10 cm of snow and Samuel was very ill, so we decided to take him to the hospital. It was a Sunday afternoon, and he had a fever of 40°C; we had to take him on the bus to get to the hospital. It was very scary for us seeing our little baby so ill. We had a four-hour wait before he was examined as there was only one doctor on duty in the emergency ward. The doctor examined him thoroughly and then finally checked his ears. I was convinced he had an ear infection by the way he was turning his head. I remembered when I was younger how my rabbit had behaved similarly when he had an ear infection. He would tilt his head sideways and try to twist it around.

My suspicions were confirmed; Samuel was suffering from a severe ear infection. We were so thankful that we were in a country where we could easily obtain medication. He was prescribed two antibiotics and other medications and the following day had greatly improved.

After the Christmas period, Paul managed to find some translation work for the first two months of the year. It didn't pay much but we were thankful to have some money coming in.

Azlan

"The prayer of a righteous man is powerful and effective."
James 5:16 (NIV)

We saw God answer our prayers once again - well we knew it wasn't only our prayers, but the prayers of those who had prayed for us over the past two years. Another miracle was about to unfold...

One Tuesday evening we specifically sensed that people were praying for us. Looking at the calendar, we were reminded that it was the day a small group of people met to pray for France and for missionaries working there. We used to lead the group when we lived in London, and knew they were undoubtedly praying for us.

As I mentioned, ever since we arrived in Lyon in May 1996, Paul had been looking for a permanent job, and apart from some small temporary jobs and his nine-month contract in Grenoble, he hadn't been offered anything else. Despite all his efforts, the doors remained tightly closed. His previous work experience did not seem enough. French qualifications appeared to be prerequisites for almost all the jobs he applied for. The previous year he had tried to sign up for a computer course to gain more skills but did not qualify for any of the training schemes that the Jobcentre ran, as only those who had previously worked in France were entitled to enrol.

In December 1997, Paul registered with the Jobcentre and applied for unemployment benefit. As I mentioned previously, he was given 75% of his previous salary per month, which kept us going. Having contributed to the social security system for over nine months, we knew that he would also be entitled to some benefits, and that his chances of getting a grant to do a training course were greater. He asked to see an advisor to find out if he qualified for help in this area. At first it looked like he would not be able to see anyone for two weeks, but 'by coincidence', somebody had cancelled a meeting that afternoon so he could speak to an advisor that same day. The advisor who met Paul was very positive when he explained why the four-month Microsoft IT Engineering course would improve his chances of finding a permanent job. She did not think, however, that she would be able to obtain approval from her superiors in time for the start of the course, which would commence in two weeks, mid-February.

The day before seeing the advisor, we were told that the Jobcentre would allocate Paul the highest possible grant, covering 80 percent of the total cost of the course. Normally it would take three weeks to process the application, but this time it only took three days. When he took the documents to Azlan (the training company), they could not believe how quickly everything had gone through. Apparently, it usually takes ten days just to get a reply! Those of you who know about French bureaucracy will know that this was truly a miracle!

The administrator at Azlan told him later that it was possible to apply for a second grant, and that he might be able to get even more of the course fees covered. He applied and managed to acquire another 15 percent more, which meant we only had to pay five percent. It was such a miracle! Paul was able to start the course on time, and after completing it he sat the first of six exams in French. Unfortunately, he failed the first one. At the time, we had a group of pastors staying with us, visiting from America. Their only reason for coming to see us was to encourage us. The Jobcentre had prepaid for all six of Paul's exams, but the condition was that if he failed one, he would have to pay to retake it. As he had failed the first exam, he had to redo it before he could sit the others, but we didn't have the money to pay for another exam. The American pastors offered to pay for him to retake it. He was then told that he could take the exams in English if he preferred to. A friend then bought the English study guides as a gift for him. He then retook his first exam and passed and went on to pass the remaining five as well. I was so proud of him. He managed to gain work experience (as part of his course requirements) with the World Health Organisation (WHO) for five weeks after the course, and we continued to pray for something permanent.

It All Hits The Fan - April 1998

"Abraham wasn't perfect. He failed, made mistakes.
But he would go back, get right with God, and then just keep
moving forward. He didn't quit when things got hard. He just
kept on going. And everywhere he went, God was there.
God was with him." Anne Graham Lotz

On top of all the difficulties that we were experiencing workwise, we started finding things difficult in our church. Before I continue, I am very much aware that if we were to find the perfect church, it would no longer be perfect the moment we joined, as no one is perfect. Duncan and Betty had been very good to us, however, sadly we had been feeling uncomfortable under their leadership for quite a while. We sometimes felt that we were being restrained from using our gifts in the church in a way that we believed God wanted us to. We were young and inexperienced in some ways, however, we know that God has given each person different gifts to enrich the church, and we felt that everything we did just wasn't quite good enough. We were criticised and corrected constantly. They also did not seem to understand the effort Paul was putting into finding work and showed him very little sympathy. They were quite hard on him at times. Once, Paul came home disillusioned after having gone specifically to meet with Duncan, hoping to get some encouragement regarding his job search. He broke down and cried. They didn't understand what it was like for Paul to be the breadwinner for our family, as they were supported financially by their church in South America and didn't need to think about where their money was coming from.

We decided to write to a pastor we trusted to ask if what we were experiencing was normal, or if it resembled "heavy shepherding". "Heavy shepherding" is a term that describes a method of psychological control, where there is unquestioning loyalty and obedience to those in church leadership. We knew that the pastor was in contact with some of the people that had come from Duncan and Betty's church, and we believed she had wisdom and experience to give us advice on how to deal with our situation. We wrote to her in confidence by email. Unfortunately, without our consent, she chose the wrong path to help us. She wrote to a contact that she knew in South America and asked him if he knew Duncan and Betty well, and if their style of leadership was something their church would agree with. He replied saying that he would get back to her. What he did next was what made it all "hit the fan". He contacted Duncan and Betty, telling them that we had written to the pastor about them; he then forwarded our email to them. Duncan and Betty then contacted us to arrange a meeting. They also told us to expect a visit from their pastor who had booked a flight to France to meet with us.

At the end of April 1998, we met with him, and it was decided that it was not going to work for us to stay in their church. We were asked to leave, and we were devastated! We wrote to our pastor in London explaining what had happened, and he suggested that we leave France and return to the UK. He felt we needed emotional healing from this breakdown and thought it would be best for us to return. We prayed about it. We had spoken to many British missionaries who had come to work in France, and incredibly, most of them had experienced something similar where they had fallen out with the people they had been working with and had to return home. We decided that as we believed God had called us to France, He would heal us emotionally where we were - so we decided to stay.

We started looking for another church. The following weekend, we visited a church in Macon, just one hour from Lyon. We prayed that someone would invite us for lunch, and that in some way, if we were invited, we would be a blessing to them. A friendly couple welcomed us into the church and invited us to have lunch with them after the service. We noticed that they didn't have children, and the subject was brought up by them later in the day that they hadn't been able to conceive. Rositta was already 38, so time was ticking for her to be able to have a child. We told them that we would pray for them on a regular basis and asked them to keep in touch with us. We went home feeling happy that we had gained new friends.

A few weeks after having left the church that we had pioneered with Duncan and Betty, we found another church in Rillieux la Pape, just outside Lyon. We decided not to serve in that church; we only wanted to attend their Sunday morning services, as spending time with other Christians helped us find emotional healing over time.

Playing Dot To Dot - May 1998

As Paul was on a full-time training course at Azlan, I was home alone with Samuel. I decided to join a mothers' and toddlers' group; I wanted to get to know other mothers, make new friends and improve my French. As Paul took his car to work, it was quite a long journey on the bus for me. I would go there once a week but didn't enjoy it much as I felt the women went only to show off their babies. They were not really interested in interacting with others. One Saturday morning, I woke up with a very itchy spot on my neck that looked like it was filled with water. Never having seen anything like it, I strangely knew what it was - chicken pox! I realised that I must have contracted it at the mothers' and toddlers' group. Knowing I was now contagious, I knew I wouldn't be able to go out again for at least two weeks. I was 28 years old, and not having contracted the disease as a young child, I had a very bad dose of it. I remember counting just the spots alone on my face - 55!! My back was unrecognisable, and I was very ill. I was still breastfeeding Samuel who was 11 months old, and yes, you guessed it, he caught it from me. It was a lot easier for him as he still didn't know how to scratch himself very well, but he had quite a dose of it too and was very niggly. The doctor prescribed a blue cream to put on the spots to stop the itching, but it was the most impractical medicine that he could have possibly given. We had to wear white clothes as the blue cream got onto everything we wore. Wearing white meant I could at least bleach the clothes afterwards. The dose of chickenpox was so bad that I was stuck indoors for three weeks. I was so relieved to finally go outside when I was finally well enough.

Samuel goes to Creche

> *"A bird sitting on a branch is never afraid of the branch breaking, because its trust is not on the branch, but on its own wings."*
> *Unknown*

Many of the French women that I met who had children seemed to work, and their children were taken to creche every day. Some babies were left there when they were just one week old! I started having funny looks from some of them when I said that Samuel had never been to a creche before. The pressure from them became too great and I began to think that perhaps I should take Samuel to a creche, and then I could, "Find a job and have a break from looking after him." I asked for advice and found a creche nearby where I felt I could trust the manager and her team to look after my child. We agreed to meet, and I took Samuel along with me so that we could both have a feel for the place and adjust to the new environment.

I left Samuel playing with the toys and the other children while we talked about how to ease him gently into the creche. She was so lovely and put her hand on my arm and told me how difficult it would be for me initially. She told me that I would feel like I was being torn away and it would be extremely tough for me to see Samuel crying when I left him. She also told me that it could take several weeks for Samuel to adjust, and I would have to remain very strong in my decision to leave him there for several hours a day. The manager said that the longer I left him, the quicker he would settle in. She asked me how I felt, and I started to cry. I had been put under so much pressure to take my child to creche when I so loved looking after him myself. I told her that I did not feel it was the right thing for him to go there, and that there was no need for him to go anyway. I believed it was the right decision for me to continue to mother my child as long as I possibly could. I thanked her for her honest advice and told her I would not be returning.

CHAPTER 7

Sing, Sing A Song

*"Every Child You Encounter
Is A Divine Appointment."*
Wesley Stafford

ROUGHLY TWO MONTHS after joining the new church, and just one month after the chicken pox, I discovered I was pregnant with our second child. I realised what a blessing it was that I wasn't already pregnant when I contracted the chickenpox. I had read somewhere that if a woman was exposed to chickenpox while pregnant, there was a chance that the developing baby could be deformed.

Two months after falling pregnant, we received the wonderful news from the couple in Macon who initially couldn't have children, that they were expecting their first baby. How wonderful to know that those long years of waiting had finally come to an end for them. I believe God rewarded them for blessing us that Sunday and providing a wonderful meal for us when things had been so tough.

Free At Last

"To forgive is to set a prisoner free and discover that the prisoner was you." Lewis B. Smedes

One year after we had left the church with Duncan and Betty, and the night before Duncan's birthday, Paul had a very vivid dream. He had an experience, like that of Jacob in the Bible. Paul felt that he had been wrestling with God, and he asked God to bless him. When he awoke, he realised that his struggle had been to do with dealing with the pain he had experienced from being rejected by Duncan and Betty and the church. The amazing thing was that he woke up pain free! That night, God had helped him deal with the pain, and he was ready to go and reconcile with them. We realised that even if they were not prepared to reconcile, we needed to do something. We had, with time, learnt where we had gone wrong. We should have spoken to them first instead of speaking to the other pastor. We knew that we didn't need Duncan and Betty to apologise to us, we simply needed to say sorry for our part, and we know that, "God makes all things work together for good."

"Then Jacob was left alone; and a Man wrestled with him until the breaking of day. Now when He saw that He did not prevail against him, He touched the socket of his hip; and the socket of Jacob's hip was out of joint as He wrestled with him. And He said, "Let Me go, for the day breaks." But he said, "I will not let You go unless You bless me!"
Genesis 32:24-26 (NLT)

Paul took some time to write a card and then we prayed before going to see Duncan and Betty that same day. It was tough standing in front of their door after such a long time. We had no idea how they were going to react, but we had to do this so that we could move on. We rang the bell, and the door opened. We were met with a hug and a smile. We were able to say sorry and we prayed with them and wished Duncan a happy birthday before leaving.

My pregnancy was going well, but when I had the second scan, the doctors thought there was something wrong with our baby's kidneys. At the third scan, they said that our baby's kidneys were enlarged. We prayed that the kidneys would be healed and decided not to be afraid but to trust God. The fourth scan at seven months said that her kidneys were now normal, and that we had nothing to worry about. We were so thankful. In March 1999, our beautiful baby Deborah was born. The nurse handed her to us neatly swaddled. It was funny not having a baby with arms and legs moving all over the place - but that was how they bundled them up in that hospital. I asked the nurse how much our baby weighed and measured. She told us that she was 3.5kg, but that they only measured babies on the third day, as they thought it was cruel to stretch them out and measure them when they had been curled up so nicely in the womb.

The birth announcement read:

"Awake, awake, Deborah! Awake, awake, sing a song!"
Judges 5:12 (NKJV)

It is with great thankfulness and joy that we
announce the birth of our daughter, Deborah,
a sister for Samuel. Born March 1999 at 10:30 am, weighing
3.430kg at Hôpital Edouard Herriot, Lyon

It was early morning on the third day that I took Deborah to see the paediatrician. Paul had not yet arrived at the hospital as he had gone home for the night. They measured her - 50 cm, weighed her again and then the paediatrician examined her. Everything was going well. She listened to her heart and then I thought the examination was over, but she listened to her heart again, listening longer this time. She looked a little worried and asked me if we had other members of our family born with heart issues. I shook my head nervously wondering what was wrong. She told me that Deborah had a hole in her heart (heart murmur) because the heart valve had not closed properly at birth. The hospital where I had given birth was not fully equipped to thoroughly test babies with heart problems, so I was told that Deborah would be transferred by ambulance to another hospital.

Just at that moment Paul arrived, not knowing anything about the examinations that had been carried out. I told him briefly what had happened and was then taken with Deborah by ambulance to another hospital. Paul couldn't come with me. I was ushered into a room where they placed Deborah on a very large bed with several machines around her. The lady looked very severe. She spoke roughly to me and then started pressing electrode pads onto Deborah's small body. She pressed hard to attach the wires to the pads and then proceeded to carry out the tests. The electrode pads did not seem to work so she ripped them off, not taking any care at all to be gentle with Deborah. I couldn't believe what was happening to our baby. Deborah started to cry and became very distressed, and the woman shouted at me asking me to pass her Deborah's dummy. "Deborah doesn't have a dummy," I said. "She is breastfed." The woman was very irritated by now and said, "Well then, I will just have to use my finger!" She shoved her finger harshly into Deborah's mouth, forcing her to suck it and stopping her briefly from crying, while she placed the new electrodes onto her tiny body. Finally, it seemed that they were correctly joined up and her test worked. I was told that Deborah would not be able to run or do any strenuous physical exercises when she was older, because of the heart murmur.

I returned home that day with Deborah to tell the news to Paul. Every time Deborah cried, she would turn blue, and it was alarming to see. Apparently, if the heart defect allows blood to cross from the right to the left side of the heart, a baby may look blue and have blue lips, as not all the blood is picking up oxygen from the lungs. Once again, we turned to Jesus and asked Him to heal Deborah's heart completely. We had to return to the hospital three months later for further tests, but the results were still the same. On top of this problem, Deborah seemed to be in pain and cried a lot after every feed. We thought it was colic, but it was more than colic and we were exhausted. We reached the stage where we had to take it in turns to hold her while she cried, and one of us would go out of the apartment for a 15-minute break just to have a few moments of silence. The doctor thought that Deborah was allergic to breast milk, so told me to stop breastfeeding and to give her formula milk. When I went to the pharmacy to buy the formula, the pharmacist asked me about my children. She could see Samuel by my side but asked if my baby was a girl or a boy. I told her it was a girl and she said, "Oh super!!" "Le choix du Roi," meaning, "The King's choice". I asked her what it meant, and she explained that it is a French expression that is used when a mother's first child is a boy, and afterwards gives birth to a girl. I couldn't help thinking that my children were God's choice - the King of Kings.

We tried the formula for a day, but she cried even more. To be honest, I thought the doctor was mistaken. How could my baby be allergic to breast milk? God had created me to be able to breastfeed, so

I decided that the doctor was wrong and continued with the breastfeeding. Two months after Deborah was born, our friend's baby in Macon was born, and they named her Tabea Deborah (named after our Deborah). The joy we had in hearing their news was overwhelming but imagine how they as parents must have felt!

The American pastors who had helped pay for Paul's exam continued to keep in touch with us and to pray for us. They had heard about Deborah and the issues she was having with her heart. There was a similar situation with a baby in their church and they prayed, believing for a double miracle. As they were unable to come and lay their hands on our daughter, (*"they will lay hands on the sick, and they will recover." Mark 16:18 (NKJV)*), they prayed over a pink cloth, following Paul's example in the Bible and sent it to us.
11 *"God did extraordinary miracles through Paul, **12** so that even handkerchiefs and aprons that had touched him were taken to the sick, and their illnesses were cured and the evil spirits left them." Acts 19:11-12 (NKJV).*

We laid the cloth on Deborah's head and believed with them that she had been healed. Her excessive crying persisted until she was one year old, but it gradually stopped without any explanation.

August 1999

"The most incredible thing about miracles is that they happen."
G.K. Chesterton

One day Paul was searching for jobs when he saw an advert for a job at Hewlett-Packard. It was asking for qualifications he didn't have. He needed to have a computer science degree but decided to apply for it as he thought he could play on the fact that he speaks four languages fluently. We could hardly believe it when he was offered the job. Before Paul started his first day at work, he mentioned to his new employer that he had already previously booked a short holiday in Die, in the Drome region in south-eastern France. They were happy for us to go.

On the first day of our holiday, mid-August, there was a total solar eclipse. We were out walking with Samuel in the field, and it went eerily quiet. The birds flew into the trees, and it became quite dark as if it was dusk. We started to walk back to our caravan, but Paul had not noticed a rabbit hole in the ground and twisted his ankle so badly that within seconds, it had swelled to more than double the size. It was shocking to see how badly sprained it was and he could hardly limp back to the car. I rushed to get the keys for the car and drove him to the hospital. They gave him a Plaster of Paris bandage and sent him on his way with a huge bag of painkillers. The nurse had to come and visit him to give him regular injections to avoid any blood clots forming. Looking after him was like having another baby in the house. As we only had a bath, it was very tricky for him to have a wash. The most unfortunate thing about this accident was that he couldn't start his new job on time. Fortunately, his new company was very good to him and patiently waited for him to get better.

When Paul was finally able to start work, he was told that as the position was newly created, he would have to recruit his own team. He advertised for the available positions and received several CVs to wade through. He couldn't believe it when he came across the CV of his instructor from the Azlan IT course that he had completed the previous year! She decided she needed a change from training people and so applied for a position at Hewlett-Packard. The incredible thing was that she was much more qualified and more experienced than Paul, and she was obviously surprised to be interviewed by him. It was a great blessing for him to have this lady join his team, as when he didn't understand something, he had someone who could help him.

CHAPTER 8

A Church to Call Home

*"Faith is permitting ourselves to be seized
by the things we do not see."*
Martin Luther

WE WERE INVITED to a church picnic where several
people from other churches were gathered for a fun
day out. We met a very kind pastor from a church in St
Jean de Bournay, (a small village one hour from Lyon),
who introduced us to his son and daughter-in law.
They spoke English quite well and seemed to want to
communicate with us in English, which was a relief for
me as I felt I could then relax and enjoy the day. We
became friends and were later invited to the pastor's
house (which was on a farm) for lunch. He told us that
his son and family would soon be leaving the area to

live in Dunkirk and wondered if we would like to replace them to help him in his church in whatever way possible. We were very excited at the prospect of once again being involved in church work. We told the pastor though, that our move to St Jean de Bournay would be for a short period of time, perhaps a couple of years, as we felt God would want us to move on again.

November 1999 - The Purchase Of Our First Home

"My home is in Heaven. I'm just traveling through this world."
Billy Graham

Paul's mom came to visit us from Holland. It was wonderful for us, and of course for our children, to have some quality time with Oma (Dutch for grandmother). Paul was in his third month of full-time employment, and we were able to relax and enjoy the moment knowing that at the end of the month, Paul would have passed the three-month trial period and would finally be employed full-time. While she was with us, Paul noticed an advert for a house for sale in St Jean de Bournay where the pastor's church was based. It was advertised in one of the real estate magazines he had picked up at work. It was a 150-year-old Bourgeois house with five bedrooms and an apartment at the back, that needed quite a bit of work. It had a big plot of land with two chestnut trees and a stream at the bottom of the garden. Paul decided to go and visit it during his lunch break. He arrived at the house to be met by a very lively cocker spaniel and was given a tour by one of the neighbours and an estate agent. He was able to take some photos and videoed the tour so that we could have a look in the evening when he returned from work. He really thought it had great potential. The following day we made an appointment so we could see it together at the weekend. On arrival, it was nothing like the house I had seen in my dream a while back, but it was amazing to think we could possibly buy our first home. My mother-in-law walked around the garden laughing. It made her so happy to think that there could be a possibility for us to buy such a place. We made an offer on the house and it was accepted, so we went to sign the initial offer at the notary's office. Paul had to show proof that he was in full-time employment, and he had to have worked for a period of three months. It was exactly three months and one day from the first day he started work. We were therefore allowed to sign the initial agreement at the end of November 1999.

Two months later, we left our apartment in Lyon and made the one-hour drive to St Jean de Bournay to start a new life there. On the motorway, traffic was building up and then we noticed a traffic sign flashing the words, "Warning, accident ahead." We started to slow down, and I left some space ahead of me, only too aware of what could happen if the traffic should suddenly halt at an unexpected time. Cars were driving dangerously close to each other and too fast also, especially knowing there was an accident ahead. We could hear a police car siren approaching rapidly from behind us driving in the fast lane - and then it happened! The traffic ahead suddenly halted and the police car which had been travelling at approximately 90 kilometres an hour, had to make an abrupt stop.

He swerved, heading in our direction and thankfully as I had left a gap in front of me, he veered into it and careered into the car in front of us, which then ploughed forward hitting probably three or four cars ahead. The car that had been hit, suddenly started smoking - perhaps from a broken radiator, and petrol seeped out from under the bonnet making it very dangerous to be near it. Images came into my mind of cars catching fire and people not being able to escape.

It was like a scene from the movies. The policeman hurriedly climbed out of his car with blood trickling down his face from his eyebrow, where he had obviously hit the windscreen, and he started shouting rapidly on his walkie-talkie, "I have just had an accident, I have just had an accident!" We were just able to pull out and move out of danger onto the emergency lane and continued driving, but my hands were shaking uncontrollably, and driving was difficult. We were very relieved that we escaped unharmed.

Welcome To St Jean de Bournay!

Upon arriving in the village, we drove past a very elderly man who was standing by the village sign which read 'St Jean de Bournay'. He waved at us several times with his beret and bowed low ushering us on. It was incredible. It was as if he was saying to us, "Welcome to St Jean de Bournay." It felt so right to be setting up home in this lovely little village, and it was special to have been welcomed in such a way.

We visited the notary, signed the final paper and the sale went through on the 12th of February 2000, and we were given the keys to our new home. It was an amazing experience being first-time buyers. The house was very cold and had two huge electric convector heaters (they looked like two huge metal boxes) which would heat up the bricks inside them overnight and churn the heat out during the day. It was a very expensive form of heating. The house had a very quirky layout. There was a beautiful carved oak staircase going up from the front door to the bedrooms. Our bedroom was at the top of the stairs on the right-hand side and overlooked the lovely garden. Opposite our bedroom was a second bedroom with an ensuite bathroom that then led to three further bedrooms. It was strange being able to walk from one room to the next without stopping. The third bedroom had a beautiful oak staircase leading down into the dining room. The dining room was surrounded by deer heads and above the fireplace was a huge boar head which had a plaque underneath which read, LEBING November 1950. We named it, "Boris the Boar".

There was a beautiful lamp hanging from the ceiling in the centre of the room above the table, which had photo frames hanging around it of hunting events dating back many years. The previous owners obviously enjoyed hunting. Just next to the front door were stairs going down to a very small cellar, where we found bottles of old walnut wine they had made. The garden looked very bare when we first arrived as it was the middle of winter.

Our house - St Jean de Bournay

The Peonie Rose

It was incredible seeing the garden come to life for the first time in the spring. It reminded me of one of my favourite childhood books, "The Secret Garden". I had never seen so many different coloured irises growing together on one pathway - nine different colours in a row. On the opposite side was an array of peonies in deep burgundy, and at the end of the pathway was a pink honeysuckle bush and a Japanese flowering quince. Two tall horse chestnut trees grew near the house that had spectacular cone-shaped pink and white flowers and surrounding them were yellow and orange daffodils with box hedging around the flower beds. There were redcurrant and blackcurrant bushes and a cherry and walnut tree too. A deep purple magnolia tree had a curved branch which was at a perfect height to sit on, and in the summer, the weeping willow at the bottom of the garden gave plenty of shade to sit under. The garden wall was covered by a wisteria vine that had cascades of purple flowers hanging like huge clusters of grapes with a strong sweet scent that you could smell all around the garden. It was wonderful watching our children, Samuel and Deborah, running around and having fun. One of their favourite things to do was to throw stones in the stream at the bottom of the garden, watching the water ripple. Thankfully the stream was fenced off. Another was to play in the two landscaped circular hedges at the centre of the garden that were at least three metres wide and almost two metres high. They could climb up the branches in the middle and pop their heads out to call us. Sometimes in the summer we saw vipers in the grass and that scared me when I mowed the lawn.

Once I was deflating a large inflatable pool that we had on the grass for the summer months so that I could put it back in the garage. When I pulled it away, a snake came out lazily and slithered off toward the stream. Thankfully the snakes that I came across seemed more frightened of me and disappeared pretty rapidly.

Your Sons And Your Daughters Shall Prophesy

"And it shall come to pass in the last days, says God, that I will pour out of My Spirit on all flesh; Your sons and your daughters shall prophesy, your young men shall see visions, your old men shall dream dreams." Acts 2:17 (NKJV)

Having joined the church in St Jean de Bournay, we continued to keep in touch with our friends from the church in Rillieux-la-Pape. We had made friends with a lovely couple who sadly had not been able to have children. Often, they would talk to us about how difficult it was not being able to conceive, and many tears were shed as it was very painful for them. We prayed for a miracle for them. One day, Samuel, Deborah and I were having breakfast together in the kitchen, and as I prayed for our day and thanked God for our food, I remembered to pray for our friends. As soon as I said "Amen," Samuel looked up and said, "They're going to have a baby soon." It sounded like a prophecy! I immediately phoned my friend to tell her what Samuel had said. She wrote it down in her diary but did not tell me where she was at that exact moment. She was in fact, on her way to Paris with her husband to talk about adopting a baby from Africa. When they arrived at the adoption office, they were told that it would be too complicated to adopt a child from abroad because of recent changes to the laws. To the agent's surprise, however, they had just been notified of a French mother who was two months pregnant and had decided to give her baby up for adoption. That meant there was still seven months to wait for the baby to be born. It was explained that once born, it was not possible to give the baby up for adoption until all the paperwork had been done, which would take approximately two months.

It was exactly nine months from the day Samuel prophesied that they would have a child, the same time it takes from conception for a mother to give birth, when they adopted their baby. They just had to wait a further two months for the paperwork to be completed and the day finally came when our friends were able to fetch their precious baby girl. God had spoken to our friends through our son, sowing a seed of hope in their hearts that day. That seed became a reality, and they became parents to a baby which so desperately needed to be loved, and oh, was she loved!!

March 2000

One year had passed since the birth of Deborah and the cardiac hospital asked us to bring her back for another examination. As there had been no further complications, we hadn't been back for several months. The time had come for her check-up, and we sat in the waiting room for a long time wondering what the outcome would be. We had prayed for Deborah's healing for one year, and it was amazing how fast time had flown. We remembered laying the cloth that had been prayed over on her head. It was finally time to take her into the examination room. I could almost hear my own heartbeat in my ears as I breathed shallowly hoping for the best news for her. The doctor carefully examined her and listened several times moving the stethoscope from side to side. He then lifted his head and smiled and said, "Your daughter has been healed!" "There is no trace of the heart murmur, and she is free to do sport; there will be no need for further examinations." What wonderful news; we praised God for her healing!!

Church Life In St Jean de Bournay

"Church is who we are, not where we go." Anonymous

We were settling in well into the church in St Jean de Bournay and we had a fantastic relationship with our pastor. He asked us to help lead worship in the church, so Paul played the guitar and sang, and I sang with him, or I played my violin. The congregation was small; there were around 20 adults and probably the same number of children. We found it very odd that these

Christians were just happy plodding along with life as usual and didn't seem in the least bit interested in inviting people from the village to church or making any effort to meet new people to talk to them about Jesus. It was sad. Most Sundays we would eat together at the farm and other people from churches nearby would be invited, and there was a large gathering. Everyone contributed bringing food to share - quiches, baguettes, salami and cheese, olives, and red wine, just to name a few. Our pastor was a very kind and caring man and often came to visit us in our house to pray with us.

A church service at the farm

Leading worship at the church in St Jean de Bournay

Mom & Dad with Samuel next to the Acanthus Spinosus

Opa and Oma with Deborah and Samuel

Japanese flowering Quince

Samuel and Deborah enjoying the garden

The Peonies and Irises

Samuel and Deborah out in the snow

The apartment at the back of our house

The dining room with "Boris the Boar"

Car Accident - April 2001

*"Decisions can be like car accidents,
quick and full of consequences."*
Allison Glock

I was seven months pregnant with our third child and was told to rest as I had some early contractions. I was also tired trying to run a big house with two small children, and no family nearby to help me. A friend had come to visit for the day, and I drove with her to the shopping centre to do my weekly shopping. On our return, a traffic jam suddenly developed under a bridge in the centre of the village. I drove through the traffic lights and slowed down and stopped under the bridge. Suddenly, we heard a car speeding towards us from behind, and then, an alarming sound of screeching brakes as it ploughed into the back of my car. We lurched forward and the seat belt pulled tightly around my big bump.

I immediately asked my friend if she was OK; thankfully we were both fine - but in shock. The man who had crashed into us clambered out of his car and came to ask if we were alright. As our cars were in an inconvenient location to be able to discuss the situation and to complete the Motor Accident Report Form, he told us that it would be a good idea to try to pull off the road onto the curb so that the other cars could get past, and we would be able to discuss the accident safely.

I eased my car forward (the back of it was very badly damaged) and parked as he had suggested. Unbelievably, the man sped off past me and I realised he was trying to escape. I started the engine quickly and drove off the curb chasing after him with my hand pressed firmly on the car horn. As I continued to press it, he eventually turned off into a parking lot. My friend meanwhile had grabbed a pen from her handbag and had written his licence plate number down, just in case we were not able to catch up with him.

Thankfully, as we turned into the parking lot, I noticed a police minibus. I went to the police officer before confronting the driver, and in my broken French explained to him what had happened. He told me that in an accident where no one was injured, the police would not usually intervene, but as I was pregnant, he decided to help me. He asked the other driver and I to climb into the minibus while my friend waited in the car. There were some chairs which he was able to turn around and we sat down at the table and started answering some questions. The police officer discovered that the man who had tried to escape, had been involved in another accident the previous day. Knowing that his insurance wouldn't pay, he tried to avoid having to pay me out of his own pocket. I was so grateful that God had looked after my friend and I, and especially that the policeman was there to help me at that time. The man had to pay for the repairs in cash, and we were so relieved that we didn't have to go through our own insurance.

An Unexpected Visit

Paul was very keen on finding out more about his Huguenot roots, and wrote to Steve Strang, the founder and publisher of the Charisma Magazine after having read an interesting article that he had written about them. Huguenots were French Protestants from the time of the Reformation, and during the Religious Wars of the 16th century, many escaped persecutions and fled to countries such as Holland, Germany, Belgium, England and South Africa.

Both Steve and Paul had traced their family roots to the Huguenot descendants. Steve replied mentioning that he had planned a trip to France to visit the place where his Huguenot ancestors had lived. He suggested coming to interview us about our life as missionaries in France, and to further discuss his family history. We were humbled that he would find the time to come and meet us in our home in St Jean de Bournay.

CHAPTER 9

A Blonde Bombshell

---

*"Let her sleep for when she wakes,
she will move mountains."*
Napoleon Bonaparte

THANKFULLY THE PREGNANCY of our third child
had gone well, although I seemed to be a lot bigger
than in my previous pregnancies (the doctor said I had
extra amniotic fluid). There were some concerns that I
had diabetes, and I was made to drink a very sickly-
sweet drink to test for this on several occasions.
Thankfully all was well. When I was six months
pregnant, I was allowed to have an 'aide ménagère' (a
home help) so that I could get more rest. Three weeks
before our baby was due, my waters broke, and I had
to go to hospital (I have a feeling the car accident

hadn't helped!). One of our friends from church who lived down the road came to pick up Samuel and Deborah. Throughout the pregnancy people had asked me if I knew what sex the baby was. I didn't but I always thought I was having a boy. On the way to the hospital, I mentioned to Paul that if it was a girl, it would be wonderful. It was always so much fun dressing Deborah up in her lovely pretty outfits. Once I was settled and in my room at the hospital, Paul decided to dash out to buy something to eat for dinner.

He was gone over two hours which was an incredibly long time, and my phone in my room hadn't been set up yet, so I could not use it to phone him (we didn't have mobile phones then ☺). I was so relieved when he eventually returned but he was looking a bit worn out! The radiator in our car had developed a leak. He had to buy a lot of water and was obliged to stop every five minutes to top it up so that the car wouldn't overheat. I was so thankful to see him. The car radiator could be fixed another time but at least he was with me to help me with the birth. Thankfully on the way to the hospital I had thought about the possibility of us having a girl. Perhaps God had prepared my heart just in time as I gave birth to a beautiful, healthy baby girl weighing 3.5kgs. I was grateful she was born three weeks early as she could have weighed a whole lot more!

The birth announcement read:

It is with great joy and thankfulness that we announce the birth of Rebecca, a sister for Samuel and Deborah. Born June 2001 at 2:35 a.m. - St Colombes-lès-Vienne, France.

"I praise you because I am fearfully and wonderfully made, your works are wonderful, I know that full well." Psalm 139:14 (NIV)

Rebecca was born with very dark hair, but it soon changed into the most beautiful, wavy, almost white-blonde hair, just like her eldest brother.

Samuel was now at school full-time but came home for lunch every day. His spoken French was progressing, and he constructed his sentences very well. Deborah was so sweet, bubbling with energy. She loved helping me with Rebecca and "cleaning" the house. Thankfully I still had a home help who came once a week. Shortly after I had given birth, I was asked to come in for the usual check-up with the gynaecologist to see if all had come back to normal. I had some burning sensations and of course didn't know what that was all about. It was revealed that I had polyps and the gynaecologist said I would have to have them surgically removed. Tests would be carried out to make sure they were benign. I went away feeling nervous, but when I was praying, I felt God give me the following Bible verses:

*"As he passed by, he saw a man blind from birth. And his
disciples asked him, "Rabbi, who sinned, this man or his
parents, that he was born blind?" Jesus answered, "It was
not that this man sinned, or his parents, but that the
works of God might be displayed in him."*
John 9: 1-3 (ESV)

I realised from reading this passage that I could ask God to heal me, and that if He did, He would get the glory. We asked Him to do just that. A few months later when I went for my next examination, all the polyps had supernaturally disappeared! There was no need to surgically remove them, and I was able to stand up in church and tell the congregation what God had done for me. I was so thankful.

A Marathon

*"We are different, in essence, from other men.
If you want to win something, run 100 meters.
If you want to experience something, run a marathon."*
Emil Zatopek

Paul was very busy with work-related studies but was still able to find the time to prepare for a marathon. He trained for just six weeks and was our hero as he finished the Lyon Marathon (42.195 kilometres) in just under five hours in the pouring rain. He could hardly walk after the race and had terrible blisters on his feet. He had been inspired to run after having met an elderly man one lunch time during work, who was training for his next marathon. The man explained that he had only started running 15 years earlier at the age of 50 and used to be a smoker. Paul decided that if a 65-year-old man, an ex-smoker, could run a marathon, there was nothing to stop him accomplishing that too (apart from himself).

Other than our involvement in leading worship at church, we also helped with the Sunday school and began leading a home Bible study group. Paul started teaching the church members how to reach out to those around them, explaining that it was not something exclusively for church leaders to do. Our church's goal was to have a home group in each of the villages that surrounded us.

We were encouraged after attending a conference in Vichy. We thoroughly enjoyed meeting leaders from all over France, including leaders from countries that had a heart for France, and who prayed on a regular basis for this nation.

CHAPTER 10

Suddenly...

*"Suddenly a sound like the blowing of
a violent wind came from heaven
and filled the whole house where
they were sitting."
Acts 2:2 (NIV)*

FOR A SIX-YEAR PERIOD we had been involved in
church planting, and during that time we had served in
many churches. Paul decided that it would be an
amazing experience for him to go to Columbia to visit
a church there that had grown from just eight members
to over 500,000 in less than 20 years. He wanted to see
if he could learn something from them and to
experience being with thousands of people
worshipping God in one place. While he was there, he
prayed and felt God tell him that it was time to start
our own church in Lyon. I had also been praying for

him while he was away and felt God tell me the same thing.

I believe that God had been preparing us for this next phase of our lives. Thankfully when we would eventually move back to Lyon, it was still feasible for Paul to commute to Hewlett-Packard where he was working, and he didn't need to look for another job

As we had made the decision to move, we started having a lot of opposition. During Paul's trip to Columbia, the children and I were sick, our washing machine broke down and the landline stopped working. Then a few days after Paul returned from Columbia, our car broke down on the motorway. The mechanic hadn't closed off the valve for the oil when he had serviced our car, and the oil poured out all over the road while we were driving. We had to make an emergency stop on the road to avoid the engine seizing. Huge lorries flew past us while we waited on the side of the road. We were there for two hours with our three small children until the tow truck arrived to pick us up and take our car away. It was a miracle that we were able to make just one short phone call to the police before the battery on our mobile phone unexpectedly ran out when we needed it the most! Despite all these things, we hadn't lost our peace or joy. All the opposition we experienced felt like confirmation that we were on the right track!

Breakthrough

We anticipated moving back into an apartment as we did not think that we would be able to afford to buy a house in the city. We looked at neighbourhoods to live in where people could easily travel to us, and where we would be able to reach out to neighbours effectively. We decided to live in the 8th arrondissement (borough) in Lyon. I still had to get over the fact that we had to sell the house that we loved so much and return to the city where things were a lot more expensive (twice as much as the village), and knowingly, properties and gardens were smaller. We made up a list of things we wanted to have in our next house: Five bedrooms, a home office, space to receive visitors, double glazing, a small garden for the children to play in, gas central heating, to name a few!

Paul gave me a list of estate agents and their phone numbers to call. Suddenly I felt very rebellious and decided I didn't want to move back at all. I sat down at the dining room table, struggling with myself to make the first phone call. I could not do it. Then something strange happened. It was as if I had fallen asleep and had a weird dream/nightmare. I could hear two people talking. One voice said, "She's not going to be able to move; she won't sell," and the other voice said, "Yes she will." "She will be able to; I know her." When I came round, I was adamant that I was not going to be stopped. I realised that the two voices I had heard were Satan and the Holy Spirit.

That day I decided to call one estate agent and told them what I was looking for. They said I would find it hard to believe, but in the neighbourhood that we were looking at, a semi-detached house had just come on the market within our budget. I understood they also had an apartment for sale with five bedrooms, but it was not located in the neighbourhood we had specified. Paul wasn't sure I had correctly understood the estate agent's descriptions, as my French wasn't that great. I told him that if I had misunderstood, he could fill the estate agent in when we met him the following day.

We arrived at the big green iron gates of number 64 rue Seignemartin. The estate agent was waiting to meet us. He unlocked the gate, and we walked in along the side of the house and found ourselves in a courtyard with a beautiful Plane tree with big green leaves and white and grey bark. There was a small cottage to the rear of the courtyard. I turned around to look at the back of the house. The elderly man who lived there had started walking down the outdoor stairs to come and meet us, but his wife stayed at the top of the balcony, resting on her arms and looking down at us. Flashback! It was exactly what I had seen in my dream four years previously. I looked at Paul with goose bumps on my arms and tears in my eyes and whispered to him, "This is it!" "This is the house I saw in my dream!"

We were amazed as it matched exactly what we had been praying for - a shop front which we could transform into a meeting room, two independent apartments we could later join up to enable us to have five bedrooms, a large basement, as well as a closed courtyard with garage and independent guest cottage. The location was perfect too. There was a bus stop just down the street, a metro station within a few minutes' walk, a tram as well as easy access to the motorway and schools just around the corner. To find a house like that in Lyon really was a miracle! We had no doubt that this was the house God had set aside for us; we signed the initial agreement to buy it that same day. I believed that God would provide everything we needed to be able to buy it.

After signing the contract, we were horrified to find out that we hadn't fully understood it. We had agreed to buy the house without the option to retract if we didn't find a mortgage or sell our house in time! Our pastor was fuming mad and could not believe what we had done. He told Paul that he was crazy for having done something like that when he had a wife and three small children to look after. He thought that we were being very irresponsible and that we were putting ourselves under extreme pressure. In normal circumstances, our pastor would have been completely right. I reassured him that it was God who had given me the dream, and that the house was exactly what I had seen in my dream. I knew God would provide. The miracles that followed were incredible. We had no savings, but the bank agreed to lend us a substantial overdraft to enable us to pay the initial five percent deposit, and another bank with which we had our first mortgage, agreed to transfer our loan onto the new house for the same low interest rate.

For Sale

We had to finance the purchase of our house in Lyon by selling our home in St Jean de Bournay in two parts. It had a partially restored small townhouse at the back and its own garden. It shared the roof with the main part of the house, but we decided to sell it separately. We started restoring it and steamed off all the old wallpaper, installed an extra window in the kitchen area and started work on putting in a new shower unit. Interest in this part of the house was greater than the main part of the house which proved more difficult to sell, as potential buyers didn't always like sharing a wall with their neighbour. We made the mistake of giving an estate agent the exclusive rights to sell our house for the first month, but had thankfully given ourselves the right to sell it as well.

CHAPTER 11

God Is Never
Too Late

*"It's never too late to be what
you might have been."*
George Eliot

WE WERE SO GRATEFUL that we had people praying for us to sell our house. We sold the townhouse ourselves to a young couple without having to pay the estate agent their commission. The estate agent had found a buyer the same day as us, but because they did not inform us immediately, they missed the boat!

The sale of the largest part of our house proved more difficult. After the agency's exclusive rights contract had expired, we were able to sign up with ten other estate agents. We also placed our own adverts in all the local shops, newspapers and on the Internet. It was very exhausting as we had at least 30 visits and had to constantly keep our house tidy. With three young children that loved spreading their toys all around the house, this certainly was very trying. Our house was almost sold five times, but each time the sale fell through because the buyers couldn't get a loan or had to sell their own properties first. Our faith and perseverance were tested.

As you can imagine we were weary and a bit apprehensive by the time the sixth couple agreed to buy the house. They had come by motorbike from Lyon after having heard that the house was for sale by word of mouth. They signed the initial sales agreement on the 23rd of May. Fortunately, they had the finances and did not change their minds, so we were able to sign the contract and the seven-day reflection period passed without them backing out. We could finally say with certainty that the house had been sold. As a sale in France roughly takes three months to be processed, it was perfect timing to enable us to move to Lyon by the end of August, just in time for Samuel and Deborah to start their new school on the 28th! Their school was just 50 meters from our new home which was so practical. The couple needed to move in by mid-September, so it all worked out very well. The sale of the two properties together was just enough to enable us to buy the house I had seen in my dream. We were able to reimburse the bank within the agreed period and had about £150 left over! It was amazing!

Those past few months had been stressful, but you can see from our experiences just how good and faithful our God is. He is never too late, but we felt had missed many opportunities to be early 😊! These difficult situations drew us closer to Him as we were learning to walk by faith.

Lyon, Here We Come!

THE NEXT CHALLENGE was that Mr and Mrs Gourand (the previous owners) were not able to get their lodgers out in time; they occupied half of the house. The Gourands also needed to wait until their new apartment was ready to move into. Thankfully they understood our predicament and allowed us to rent the upstairs part of the house while they moved into the guest cottage for two months. All our needs had been met. We arrived in Lyon on the 22nd of August.

The lodgers occupying the downstairs apartment had the right to stay in their accommodation until the end of October. The coming months promised to be eventful and hectic, but what was new? We were used to it. It was going to be interesting sharing the home that we were buying with two other families, but knowing it would just be a short time before it was finally ours, we looked forward to getting started. The vision in our hearts to start a church and see multitudes saved in Lyon motivated us enormously. With almost 99% of the French not being part of a church, there was plenty of room for expansion.

As we started packing our things into boxes, Rebecca pulled a cupboard over on top of her but miraculously didn't even have a bruise! We believe an angel kept her from being crushed. We were given the keys to the house on the 26th of September 2002. One week after moving into our new home, we had a knock on the door from our neighbours across the road. They came to invite us to their home for dinner so that we could get to know them. They had a seven-year-old daughter called Edwige whom we had seen playing outside from our window upstairs overlooking their garden. She always played on her own and we felt very sorry for her. She was so happy that her neighbours had children she could play with, and we were so grateful for the welcome we had been given from this wonderful family.

Leaving St Jean de Bournay

CHAPTER 12

Trying To Keep Up

*"I feel like I'm too busy writing
history to read it."*
Kanye West

DECEMBER 2002: Our busy lifestyle made it difficult
for us to keep in contact with our friends and prayer
partners as regularly as we would have liked to. This
past year had been extremely busy and had included
trips to Columbia, the UK, Switzerland and the
Netherlands (Christmas). We had bought our new
home in Lyon, sold our house in St Jean de Bournay
(in that order!) and started a church. We had
entertained visitors from Africa, North America and
Europe, but amidst all the chaos, we were very happy.
This was the fourth time we had moved in six years,

and it seemed to get more exhausting as we accumulated more things with each move. This time we needed professional help. We had a huge removal truck with a trailer and four men to help move everything. This was done over a two-day period where we finally exchanged the countryside for the city. I don't think anyone gets used to moving.

French Presidential Elections 2002

At the beginning of 2002, just before the elections, thousands of believers in France and around the world were praying for a spiritual breakthrough. Many believe that the outcome of the elections was a direct answer to those prayers. In the first round, the extreme right gained second position, and to prevent them from going any further, the Socialists and Communists were obliged to encourage their voters to vote for the Conservative candidate - their main opponent, who ultimately won the elections. Imagine their humiliation! Politics has become very divisive.

The only solution that can change the social divisions in our societies is the Gospel of Jesus Christ. God became man so that we can know His love, presence and life-transforming power. This has been true for 2000 years and it is still true today. France needs God more than ever. We felt that Europe, and especially France, was rapidly drifting away from its Christian roots. Violence, social unrest, the breakdown of the family and unemployment all add to the sense of hopelessness and despair. If ever there was a right time for God to break into this spiritual vacuum, it is now.

Centre Chrétien International

In our new home we started almost immediately preparing the shop front by knocking down walls and preparing our meeting room. The room was 40 metres squared, a perfect size to begin our Sunday morning meetings as well as running Alpha courses during the week. The Alpha course is an evangelistic course which consists of 12 weekly meetings that begin with a dinner. There are a series of talks, addressing key issues relating to the Christian faith.

We called our church 'Centre Chrétien International' and had to begin the process of registering it with the authorities. We also subscribed to a legal advice service provided by an organisation specialising in assisting churches with the legal paperwork. Keeping up with the French legislation was a full-time job. Many Evangelical churches in France are considered to be cults, and evangelism, which is seen as proselytising, is forbidden by Law and can be punished with a prison sentence. In many people's minds, churches are out to get money from people, so we knew it was vital that our papers for our church were in order.

New Kids On The Block

Our three children adjusted very well to moving from the countryside back into the city and were a great help with the move. We were very happy to be back in Lyon again, and the contact we had with people seemed to be more spontaneous. I became acquainted with many mothers from the neighbourhood and tried to get to know our neighbours as well. Our neighbour's daughter started coming regularly to our house and loved hearing stories about Jesus. She asked us to pray for her when we prayed for our children which was so lovely.

Samuel (five and a half years old) was in his third year at school and spoke French well. He often corrected our English accents when we spoke in French. He enjoyed reading, looking after his sisters and telling the other children in his class what to do. We were delighted when in October that year he asked the Lord Jesus to come into his heart. We saw a big change in him; he began to realise when he was naughty or was disobedient and tried his best to be good.

Deborah (three and a half years old) was at the stage where she enjoyed playing with her dolls. She started school for the first time in September and loved it. Before that she didn't really speak any French but seemed to understand quite a lot.

Rebecca (18 months), the blondest of the lot, was a very active little girl and kept us running around the whole day and sometimes even at night. She always seemed to know what she wanted and kept her eldest brother and sister entertained. We found out that she was born with slightly bandy legs, but it did not seem to bother her.

One day Rebecca decided to sit outside in the sunshine, and without me seeing her, took her little wooden chair with her down the concrete stairs that led to the courtyard below. She missed a step and fell almost all the way down to the bottom of the stairs landing very badly on her face. The screaming that came from her was enough to wake the whole neighbourhood. I ran as fast as I could. Her face was badly scraped, and her forehead had a huge bump on it (the French call it an 'oeuf de pigeon' - a pigeon's egg). It was so big that her right eye could only see partially as the bump blocked her vision. It was a very traumatic time. I looked for all the symptoms but as she didn't lose consciousness or vomit, we decided not to rush her to the hospital, but to nurse her ourselves. A few days later, Deborah was out playing in the courtyard. She climbed up onto the windowsill to sit and swing her legs. When she decided to get down, her little legs were too short to reach the ground and she toppled over and also landed on her face, badly grazing her nose. It was terrible taking the children to school as everyone could see their faces and it looked like they had been beaten up.

As with all children, we had the usual coughs and colds, but Deborah seemed to be having quite an unusual amount of them. We tried all sorts of things to help her. Lots of fresh fruit and nose drops, but nothing seemed to help. She was eventually examined by a specialist to find that her adenoids were so big that they were blocking her nasal passages. In April 2003 I drove Deborah to the "Infirmerie Protestante de Lyon" hospital to have her adenoids taken out. The doctor had told me not to worry and reassured me that I would be there with Deborah when she was put to sleep, and that I would be there when she awoke from the anaesthetic. I told Deborah that she was going to have a small operation on her nose. I mentioned it would be a bit sore, but I would be by her side and would hold her hand. The doctor came in and put an anaesthesia mask on her face while she lay on the hospital bed. We waited for a long time and were told that the previous patient had taken much longer than expected. To speed things up, they decided they would have to take Deborah in without me being there. She was not asleep by that stage, but the anaesthetic she had been breathing in, had made her calm and sleepy. As soon as she had been wheeled out of the room, I could not help but cry. I had told her that I would be with her and what the doctor had said was wrong. The time dragged on, and I must have waited over an hour. Suddenly, I recognised Deborah's cry. She had woken up quicker than they had thought and was crying very loudly down the corridor. It echoed everywhere - you know the sound you get in the hospital corridors. Once again, I wasn't there when she woke up and I felt dreadful about it. Blood was leaking out of her nostrils, and I felt so sorry for her. She was so brave, and I was incredibly proud of her. The operation was a success and after several hours we were released to go home.

CHAPTER 13

The Speedy
Arrival

*"How can there be too many children?
That's like saying there are
too many flowers."*
Mother Teresa

SIX MONTHS AFTER ARRIVING in our new home
in Lyon, I discovered that I was pregnant with our
fourth child. It had not been as easy to conceive this
time, but the pregnancy was going well. During this
time, and with the help of some builders, we did an
enormous amount of building work on our home. We
knocked down walls, did tiling and installed a new
staircase. We demolished the kitchen that was on the

first floor, transformed it into Samuel's bedroom and fitted a new kitchen downstairs. We had unfortunately hired a builder who was very unreliable. He had been recommended to us by a friend, but we found out later that he was in debt and couldn't pay his workers. One of his workers was an excellent tiler. He had started to do some work in our house but hadn't completed it. He told us that he wasn't coming back because he had not been paid. We had already paid the building company an advance, which was much more than the work that had been carried out. We were so frustrated at the thought of losing the tiler that we suggested we would pay him cash and deduct what we had paid him from the final bill. He agreed to stay. We paid him, but then he had a terrible argument with the builder and threatened to walk out. I then stepped in. I knew that the tiler was having issues with his wife and was having to go to court to sort a matter out later that day. Heavily pregnant, I ran and grabbed hold of his papers that he had left lying on top of his jacket and told him that he wasn't going anywhere until he had completed what we had paid him to do. I told him that the situation was causing me a lot of stress which was not good for me being pregnant. He went back to do the tiling and worked until it was lunchtime and then he went out for a break. What was I to do? He needed a break, but I had my doubts as to whether he would return. I was right; he walked out, and we never saw him again. We lost a lot of money as the builder also walked out on us, and we had no alternative but to find another company to complete the work. This time we made sure that we signed a contract and insisted it included a completion date and penalties for late delivery.

As I had been feeling so stressed during the pregnancy, we prayed each night over our baby and talked to him. We told him that even though we were having a difficult time, we were not annoyed at him, but were looking forward to seeing him and loved him very much. We prayed for him to be a child that was very content and peaceful and not at all affected by our bad experiences. My mother-in-law came to visit us from Holland, arriving a few weeks before the due date. She thought that as we were expecting our fourth child, he would be born early, and it would be best to come well in advance. I started having contractions, but they did not do anything, so the nurse sent me home after giving me medication to stop them. She explained that if the contractions were the real ones, nothing would stop them. I was also told not to come back to the hospital until the contractions came every five minutes.

Two days after that, the contractions came faster and more intensively. My first contraction was so painful that I decided to sit in the bath just to ease the pain. I tried running the water, but for some reason the water wouldn't warm up. The second contraction came three minutes later and then every three minutes after that. I hurriedly dressed and went to wake up Paul's mom who was staying in the cottage in our courtyard. She came across to stay with the children and rested on our bed. I didn't have time to put on my shoes. We hurried into the car and Paul raced to get us to the hospital. Thankfully the hospital was only a five-minute drive away, and I told him not to stop at any red traffic lights, as I thought there was a possibility that our baby would be born in the car. We arrived at the hospital, and I could hardly walk because of the contractions. The nurse rushed me in to examine me; I was seven and a half centimetres dilated and there was no time to wait! I was taken immediately into the labour ward, was put on the bed and asked if I would mind if a student midwife attended - I didn't. The midwife showed me where the buzzer was if I needed to call her and ran off to do something. She was gone just a few minutes when I felt that our baby was going to be born. I told Paul and he ran to the corridor and shouted for her. She came running back into the room with the student midwife and only had time to put on one glove when our fourth child was born.

The birth announcement read:

It is with great joy and thankfulness that we announce the birth of Joshua, a brother for Samuel, Deborah and Rebecca.

Born December 2003 at 2:40 am weighing 3.640kgs at Edouard Herriot, Lyon

*"Have I not commanded you? Be strong and courageous.
Do not be afraid; do not be discouraged, for the Lord
your God will be with you wherever you go."*

Joshua 1:9 (NIV)

Three days after Joshua was born, the photographer came into my room to take some photographs of us. She took him out of his cot and laid him on the bed. He was dressed in his little Christmas reindeer suit. As she laid him on the bed, his hands lay open in a very relaxed manner. She immediately commented. "What a peaceful baby you have!" "Normally when I place babies down on the bed, their fists clench up and they throw their arms back above their heads and take a while to settle." "Your baby is just so incredibly peaceful which is so lovely to see." It was then that I remembered! God had answered our prayers and our beautiful baby boy had not been affected by the stress that I had experienced during my pregnancy. It was so noticeable that the photographer had commented, and she had the experience to be able to do so!

Wave It Goodbye

Our amazing seven-year-old microwave suddenly stopped working one day. We had bought it in the UK before we left for France. I suppose it was not surprising that it had finally given up, as I had used it a lot with our big family. We didn't have the money to buy a new one, so we took it to the shops to get it repaired. After three weeks and no response, I phoned to find out whether it was ready to collect. I was told that they were unable to obtain the spare parts to repair it, and they asked me if I wanted them to dispose of it. I wanted to see if there would be another possibility of repairing it, so we went to collect it. When we brought it home, I asked Paul to come with me into the kitchen to pray over it, asking God to repair it for us. We both laid hands on it and prayed. We then plugged it back in and tested it. The amazing thing was that not only was it functioning well, but the light bulb which had blown five years previously, was working again!

An Unwelcome Visit

"Too many Christians have a commitment of convenience. They'll stay faithful as long as it's safe and it doesn't involve risk, rejection, or criticism. Instead of standing alone in the face of challenge or temptation, they check to see which way their friends are going." Charles Stanley

We decided to visit the only church in our neighbourhood to introduce ourselves and to tell them what we were hoping to do as a church. We went there one Sunday morning and spoke to the pastor briefly, mentioning where we lived. He looked surprised and a little annoyed but told us that he would like to meet with us. We invited him to our home that week and he arrived with four other elders from his church. Apprehensively we shared with them how God had miraculously enabled us to buy the house. I explained the details of the dream I had long before we had any money to buy a house. We told them that we had not moved into their neighbourhood to encourage members from their church to come to our meetings, but we wanted to reach out to people living in the council estate tower blocks nearby and believed that God had sent us there. Their congregation consisted mainly of people who lived in the suburbs, and they would drive into the city. Unbelievably these church leaders were very angry with us that we had moved into their vicinity, and one of them started shouting at us. As soon as he started shouting, Samuel and Deborah came down the stairs to ask us why he was so angry. I turned to the church leaders and asked in my best French the following question, "How can I explain to our children that you are angry with us because we want to see people become Christians in our neighbourhood?" They did not know what to say but asked us whether we would still have moved into the area if we had been part of the same denomination as them. The answer was obvious. God had given me the dream and had provided for the house, so it was a big "Yes" from us! They responded by telling us that we were not welcome in the neighbourhood and told us to return to the UK. They then stood up from the table to leave, and one of them said, "When I get to heaven, I will be surprised if I see you there." It was very sad to see how insular they had become as a church, and we were so shocked to have been treated in that way.

Bits And Bobs

*"If you want something you've never had, you must
be willing to do something you've never done."*
Thomas Jefferson

Even though the electricity and heating were in
working order when we bought the house, there were
three independent accommodations initially and we
needed to regroup the electrical switchboard and install
a new central heating system. Paul bought a book to
teach himself how to replace all the old electricity
cables, and amazingly managed to rewire the house and
stay alive! It was hard work with small children as they
sometimes tried to help in their own way, which was
cute, but they somewhat slowed us down. When the
American evangelist Benny Hinn came to France, Paul
was invited to serve as a steward and translator during
his meeting in Marseille. There were many people that
attended, and Paul was asked to be on the watch for
any strange people who had come to disrupt the
meeting. Hundreds came forward for salvation and
many experienced supernatural healings in their
bodies. It was encouraging to see so many Christians
together in one meeting.

Knocking down the walls in rue Seignemartin

CHAPTER 14

The French Connection

*"We make a living by what we get but
we make a life by what we give."*
Winston Churchill

DECEMBER 2004. It was just over two years since
we had returned to Lyon. We were grateful for the
progress that had been made. Making our home
liveable and ready to receive visitors took most of our
energy; our house and courtyard resembled a building
site for a very long time. We were finally ready and
could now use all the rooms in the house, and most
importantly, the spacious front room which we used
for welcoming visitors and doing a number of other

activities. Before a house is built it needs to have good foundations, and the same is true for starting a church.

It was important to have a spiritual foundation of prayer and intercession, faith and vision. Prayer is to our lives, what fuel is to an engine. We will not go very far in life without a healthy prayer life. Intercession is a step up from prayer. Intercession is praying God's heart into a specific situation or standing in the gap on behalf of a person or region in need of mercy and grace. We believed God had called us to do this even though we often felt very inadequate and overwhelmed by this challenge. We had our share of frustrations and disappointments but knew that what we were doing had a purpose and was worth the effort. There is nothing more worthwhile in life than to see people's lives transformed as they come to know God. After the birth of Joshua, we decided we needed a break from all the building work and put it on hold for three months to allow ourselves time to adapt to having another baby. In the Spring we plucked up the courage to finish off some loose ends on the house that had not been completed by our builders. During the summer months my parents visited for two months and with a lot of help from my dad, we were able to advance notably on the renovations.

We continued to get to know people in our neighbourhood on a more personal level, mainly through the local school that our children attended, but they still seemed a bit distant. We realised that to win people's hearts, it was important to find practical ways to help them. The Church in the West, and especially in France has had a credibility problem with non-believers for a long time. The French can be suspicious and often question people's motives. In an effort to build bridges, we wanted to show that we were not in the business of asking, but in the business of giving. "For God so loved the world that He gave..."

When we used to live in London, Paul worked for a Christian charity called Pecan. This charity has trained thousands of unemployed people in job search skills or introduced them to vocational training. Using the experience Paul gained while working for them, we decided to start something similar aiming to reach out to people in our neighbourhood. That summer we started a computer course in our home. We named the course AILES (the French word for "wings"). Our slogan was, "Discover new horizons with WINGS." Every Monday evening, we set up several laptops in our lounge. We taught basic computer skills such as word processing and sending and receiving emails, and we also helped them with their job searches. We had eight people attending on a regular basis, many of them of North African background. They appreciated the fact that we offered this course free of charge. Most of the people that attended came through personal invitation. Unemployment has been a big social problem for many years and in a small way, we wanted to help. We knew from experience how discouraging it could be to be turned down for a job and to feel unqualified. Even though finding a good job is very important, what is more important, is to discover your purpose in life. We work to live, but we shouldn't live to work. If we don't live to work, what do we live for? This is one of the most important questions in life and if we fail to answer it correctly, we will be unfulfilled, frustrated and miss the mark. Our purpose is the God-given destiny that He has put inside of us, and we give glory to God by fulfilling our purpose. With this in mind, we hoped to invite the people attending the computer course to an Alpha course in our home and decided we would start at the beginning of the New Year.

At the end of December 2004, 20 children attended a Christmas party for a Bible club in our house. We had invited a friend to help teach the children. We were so excited to have the opportunity to be able to freely speak to them about the true meaning of Christmas, as most of them hadn't heard it before. It was such a fun afternoon for all of us.

Christian Bible club hosted in our home

We also organised a Christmas party and invited everyone who had attended the computer course that year. We decided to offer them all a copy of the Jesus video which included the New Testament and a tract as a Christmas gift. We talked to them about the Alpha course that we had decided to run in the New Year, mentioning that we would still be continuing the computer course. Immediately we saw fear in their eyes, and there was a terrible uneasiness in the room. They looked at each other and then at us, thanked us for the coffee and said that they would not be returning for the computer course, nor the Alpha course! We were so shocked at their reaction. Later that week, one of them returned to thank us discreetly. He told us that he thought we were lovely people but explained that in France many people are afraid of cults. This was the reason why everyone left in a hurry - believing we were either part of a cult, or that we were starting one. He also told us that he had spoken to one of the mothers whose son had come to the Christmas children's Bible club. She said that as she was a Muslim, she would not allow him to come back to our home for any other children's Bible club meetings. It was a huge disappointment. Apart from personal witnessing, the Alpha course was the tool we wanted to use to present the Gospel in a relevant way. It was back to the drawing board!

In January we started our first Alpha course. We put an advert in the Lyon newspaper and it was placed in between the headings "Clairvoyants" and "Dating Agencies"! We also distributed 400 handwritten invitations around our neighbourhood. Only two people responded to our advert - one of them, a full-time clairvoyant! Five people attended the course. When I first heard that a clairvoyant was interested in attending, I felt afraid. I was a young Christian and hadn't any experience with people involved in the occult. I initially asked God to stop him coming, but then realised that I wasn't praying the right prayer. I then asked people to pray with us that if God wanted him there that he would come. I asked God to give us wisdom to know how to deal with him, and that his life would be impacted by attending the Alpha course. I also prayed that our family and home would be protected. In the morning, knowing that the first session would take place that evening, I spent time praying and God gave me this Bible verse:

"The LORD is my strength and my shield; my heart trusts in him, and he helps me. My heart leaps for joy, and with my song I praise him." Psalm 28:7 (NIV)

Another translation says:

"The Lord is my strength and my breastplate, my heart had faith in him and I am helped; for this cause my heart is full of rapture, and I will give him praise in my song." Psalm 28:7 (BBE)

When Paul opened the door and the clairvoyant gentleman walked in, I could feel fear rising inside me again and felt light-headed. I told Paul that I needed to go to the kitchen. I excused myself and went to pray. "God, You have allowed this man to come here, so please remove any fear that I am feeling right now, protect us and give me peace." As I prayed, I experienced a very strange thing. I could feel something cold, as if a cold metal breastplate had been inserted into my chest! I knew I was sensing what the Bible calls a "breastplate of righteousness", which is part of the armour God gives to protect us as Christians. I was then reminded of the verse that He had given me in the morning and knew that everything would be alright.

The Armour of God

"Finally, be strong in the Lord and in his mighty power. Put on the full armour of God, so that you can take your stand against the devil's schemes. For our struggle is not against flesh

and blood, but against the rulers, against the authorities, against the powers of this dark world and against the spiritual forces of evil in the heavenly realms. Therefore, put on the full armour of God, so that when the day of evil comes, you may be able to stand your ground, and after you have done everything, to stand. Stand firm then, with the belt of truth buckled around your waist, with the breastplate of righteousness in place, and with your feet fitted with the readiness that comes from the gospel of peace. In addition to all this, take up the shield of faith, with which you can extinguish all the flaming arrows of the evil one. Take the helmet of salvation and the sword of the Spirit, which is the word of God. And pray in the Spirit on all occasions with all kinds of prayers and requests. With this in mind, be alert and always keep on praying for all the Lord's people." Ephesian 6:10-18 (NIV)

I felt strength come into me and was filled with peace. I reassured Paul that the man was meant to be there, and that God would help us. It was clear that this man had come with his own agenda at first, as he was trying to recruit us and the others attending the course, for some of his seances. He also brought along with him some recordings of his own New Age music and asked us to play it in our home. We were polite, but firm and told him that we would be playing our own Christian music, and that he should not come to our meetings with other motives in mind. The first two evenings he seemed to be very tense. However, he kept coming and slowly we saw him relax and enjoy talking with us and having the possibility of asking questions. One session that we ran troubled us a lot. We were sitting behind him listening together to the Alpha video - the speaker was teaching on being filled with the Holy Spirit. Suddenly, we saw something moving inside the man's back, as if a snake was slithering inside him. Paul and I both looked at each other and mouthed the same word "snake". In the Bible there is a story about the Apostle Paul encountering a slave girl, possessed with a spirit of divination, or as another translation puts it, as someone who has a "spirit of clairvoyance". Another translation says that she had a "spirit of Python":

"One day as we were going to the place of prayer, we were met by a slave girl with a spirit of clairvoyance, who earned a large income for her masters by fortune-telling."
Acts 16:16 (BSB)

"Now it happened of us going to the place of prayer, a certain girl, having a spirit of Python, met us, who was bringing her masters much gain by fortune-telling."
Acts 16:16 (BLB)

It appeared that this man was under the influence of an evil spirit because of what he had been practicing. Sadly, he only came to seven sessions, perhaps because he was so deeply involved in his occultic practises. We were happy that he came, that he heard just how much Jesus loved him, and that he had the Word of God spoken into his life. Another man who came on the course shared that for most of his married life he was filled with shame, guilt and terrible sadness. His wife had aborted one of their children as they were afraid that they could not afford to keep it. He did not think God would ever forgive him for that. We were able to comfort him by telling him that God had indeed forgiven him, and that one day he would be able to meet his child in Heaven. We saw such a positive change in this lovely man, and instead of sadness, hope. It was so wonderful that we had been able to help him.

Those that attended loved the Alpha course and asked if there were any other courses they could do; they appreciated the friendly environment, fellowship with other Christians and discussing the Bible. Even though only a few people responded to our 400 invites, we were not discouraged. There is a story about a little boy and how he was able to make a difference to his environment; I thought I would share it with you:

The Boy And The Starfish

A man was walking along a deserted beach at sunset and noticed a young boy in the distance. As he drew nearer, he saw that the boy kept bending down, picking something up and throwing it into the water. Time and again he kept hurling things into the ocean. As the man approached, he was able to see that the boy was picking up starfish that had been washed up on the beach, and one at a time, he was throwing them back into the water.

The man asked the boy what he was doing, and the boy replied, "I am throwing these washed-up starfish back into the ocean, or else they will die through lack of oxygen." "But, said the man, you can't possibly save them all, there are thousands on this beach, and this must be happening on hundreds of beaches along the coast." "You can't possibly make a difference."

The boy looked down frowning for a moment, then bent down to pick up another starfish. Smiling, he threw it back into the sea and replied, "I made a huge difference to that one!"

Transformed Lives

Following the Alpha course, our friend Patrick, whom we had known for nine years, recommitted his life to God and decided to get baptised. His baptism took place in a church nearby and we were so excited as he was the first person we had baptised since our arrival in France.

As an indirect result of the Alpha course, a Portuguese friend of ours that we had met when we first arrived also became a Christian. She used to be our neighbour. We spoke to her about God on many occasions and answered her questions. We invited her to the course, but she was unable to attend. I was able to help her pray to invite Jesus into her life. What a happy day that was!

"That's the way God responds every time one lost sinner repents and turns to him. He says to all his angels, 'Let's have a joyous celebration, for that one who was lost I have found!"
Luke 15:10-12 (TPT)

CHAPTER 15

"The Longer The Wait, The Greater the Reward."

"The only man I envy is the man who has not yet been to Africa - for he has so much to look forward to."
Richard Mullin

AFTER 11 YEARS of waiting, we were finally able to afford a two-week holiday in Zimbabwe. "11 years?!" Can you imagine how difficult that was for me not being able to return to my home country for that long? It was tough, but God had given me the strength to endure the long wait. It had become extremely difficult for my relatives to continue living there, and we were not sure how much longer they would be able to cope.

I longed to show our children where I was brought up, and to help them understand a bit of my own culture. The children were so excited that they would be able to see the big animals in the wild, and that they would have the possibility of climbing the trees in Granny and Grandad's garden.

Knowing it would be a long flight with four children under the age of seven, we prayed for favour with the flight attendants to obtain the best possible seats. We were told that as we had four young children, we would be allowed on the plane earlier than the other passengers. We were led down a long passageway and were told to wait briefly before boarding the plane. Just at that moment, a Zimbabwean lady came screaming down the corridor, accompanied by two officials, and was taken onto the plane ahead of us. Sadly, she was not allowed to live in the UK and had to return to Zimbabwe. It made me realise how blessed I was to be able to live in Europe; it was only possible because my dad was born in England.

We were finally ushered onto the plane. As Joshua was still under the age of one, he should have been allocated a cot to sleep in, but there weren't any available. We were therefore told that we could be upgraded to Business Class. We were moved to another area where the seats were much more spacious, and our children were given the best toys I had ever seen on a flight. Joshua was given a wind-up soft aeroplane, and the others had hand-held electronic games to play with.

On arrival in Zimbabwe, we were lent a six-seater car to drive by the pastor of the church I used to attend in Harare. We were able to visit several game reserves and spent quality time with my parents at the home where I used to live. We drove to the different schools I went to and showed our children the company I used to work for. It was wonderful for me to see my children running around the garden I had played in when I was younger. They discovered "chongololos" (an African millipede), chameleons, army ants and other insects. We had the opportunity to ride on an elephant (a first time for us all) and while canoeing, we kept a keen eye out for crocodiles, and of course did our best to tan in the sun.

We especially enjoyed the opportunities to share with many Christians there. My church in Harare invited us to talk about what we were doing in France, and Paul was asked to preach at their Sunday afternoon church service. The country was still as beautiful as ever, but the economic and political situation was desperate. Despite the enormous challenges the country faces, most people there realise that the answers in life are not found in man, but only in a relationship with God. While driving around Harare we saw that there was a church on almost every street corner.

Since 1992, the number of churches in Zimbabwe had more than doubled and there is now one church for every 600 inhabitants. Before we left to go to Zimbabwe on holiday, we had the opportunity of meeting the representative of the Evangelical churches in Lyon. He told us that Greater Lyon (encompassing the city of Lyon and most of its suburbs), which has more than 1.5 million inhabitants, had no more than 40 churches and less than 5,000 members in total. There is one Evangelical church for every 60,000 people in France. The difference between Zimbabwe and France is like night and day.

"Then he said to his disciples, "The harvest is plentiful but the workers are few. Ask the Lord of the harvest, therefore, to send out workers into his harvest field." Matthew 9:37-38 (NIV)

When it was time to leave Harare, it felt like we had been there longer than two weeks. We had done so many things and had seen a lot of family members and friends; it was wonderful. Unfortunately, Rebecca had picked up a nasty flu bug on the last day and was coughing a lot. When we had finally said our goodbyes to everyone, and had cried our last tears, we hoped to be able to relax on the flight. Unfortunately, Rebecca's coughing worsened. No matter what we tried, we just couldn't stop our little one from coughing! A lady behind kindly offered a cough sweet to try to help, but as she sucked it, she inhaled some saliva and that made it worse. Finally, in frustration, a man sitting behind Rebecca lashed out and slapped her on her arm; he was really irritated by her coughing. Thinking back, I should have done something and reported him, but we were all too exhausted. Finally, she fell asleep.

An hour before landing in London we could see snow-capped mountains; snow seemed to be everywhere. We were told that our connecting flight from London to Lyon would be delayed for several hours because of the snow. We waited five hours for the plane to arrive, and thankfully it did, as we were told ours would be the last one that would be allowed to take off because of the poor weather conditions. Exhausted, the children fell asleep again on the next flight, and when we finally landed in Lyon, we struggled to wake them.

It was so difficult as the three eldest children all had to help carry something. We were so glad to finally arrive home, and we collapsed into our beds at 2:30 am. After the pleasant weather in Harare, the bitterly cold temperatures of -6° Celsius was a shock to our system. The following day Deborah saw that I was sad, and at lunchtime she brought me a photo of my mom and dad and put it in front of me while we were eating; it was so sweet.

CHAPTER 16

Life At School
Has Its Challenges

*"Dear Mom, you get mad at me for not
acting my age, and then start crying
because I'm "growing up too fast."
Sincerely, pick one!"*
Unknown

MARCH 2005: As we now had three children in
school, we prayed even more for them; we also prayed
for their teachers. Balancing family, work and church
life wasn't an easy task, and it was comforting knowing
that others were praying for us all. We knew that our
children could easily be influenced by others in their

classes; quite a few of the children were from very needy families.

Deborah was at the age where she loved anything pretty and especially if it sparkled. She thoroughly enjoyed going to school, but could not read or write, although she could write her name. Rebecca's first experience in school proved to be a big challenge. She didn't speak French and understood very little. She had to sit still in class when the teacher read stories, which for an active and boisterous three-year-old who didn't understand a word, wasn't very easy! Nevertheless, she was able to quickly learn the colours, and could count to six in French. Joshua had just begun to stand up by himself and was always very amused by his brother and sisters. They loved making him laugh and he took everything in with great attention, chuckling away at the sight of the fluffy toys they danced in front of him. He also loved seeing dogs and cats when we were out and about. The children in Samuel's class had nicknamed him "Prof d'anglais" (the English Professor). Obviously, it was because he could speak English fluently and was now becoming bilingual; it made me smile. Samuel, however, was unfortunately picking up some of the swear words that the children in the courtyard were using. Of course, he had no idea what he was saying but just thought it sounded cool. His teacher had to tell him that if he didn't hear her use those words, then they were words that shouldn't be repeated.

Samuel's first primary school teacher introduced yoga in her class under the guise of "relaxation exercises" which we were not happy about. This article explains why we don't agree with it:

Dr George Alexander, who taught World Religions at Biola University, was born in Sri Lanka and grew up in India, the birthplace of Hinduism and yoga. He states that yoga poses are actually offerings to the 330 million Hindu gods.

"Many Westerners who practice yoga today are unaware that the physical positions assumed in yoga, symbolizes a spiritual act: worshiping one of the many Hindu gods," Dr Alexander said. "To a Hindu, yoga is the outward physical expression of a deep spiritual belief. You cannot separate one from the other." Since yoga is tied so strongly to Hinduism, can there be such a thing as "Christian yoga," or would that be an oxymoron (a contradiction in terms)? Many practicing Hindus, as well as many Christians, agree that since yoga is Hinduism, the two cannot be combined. Missionaries on trips to India have often seen people performing yoga poses in front of statues of the gods in the streets. Some brought offerings of flowers, some brought fruit and some brought themselves. The Bible clearly tells us to stay away from this in the following Bible verse: Acts 15:29 "abstain from things offered to idols." (3)

We arranged a meeting with Samuel's teacher, Madame Moulin (Mrs Mill), to talk about our concerns and she agreed to take him out of that class each week. She explained, however, that there was a great need for children to have yoga relaxation classes as she believed it would help them to calm down. We found it difficult to believe (regardless of what relaxation lessons she was teaching), that on a Monday morning after a weekend there would be a need for relaxation classes! The following week, when I was looking in Samuel's rucksack to see if he had any homework, I found a little notebook I hadn't seen before. I took it out and flicked through the pages. There were some very strange looking pictures that he had drawn of spaced-out looking children lying on the ground. When I asked him what he had drawn, he told me that the teacher had kept him in the classroom and had asked him to draw what was happening to the children during the yoga lesson. He explained that when they did yoga, they looked like kittens that had been picked up by the scruff of their necks and looked limp! Once again, we had to see the teacher to ask her to take Samuel out of the classroom during her yoga lessons.

Madame Moulin also used to frighten Samuel and the others in his class with her Mona Lisa picture that she kept hidden behind the blackboard in her classroom. When she had to briefly go out of the classroom, she would fold back one of the blackboards at the front of the class, revealing a picture of Mona Lisa. She would say, "She's looking at you and can see everything you are doing while I am out!" On another occasion, Samuel was asked by her to learn a poem about a witch. The witch was trying to catch a baby boy to chop him up and make a stew for dinner. As Samuel's little brother was only one year old, this really disturbed him, and he started having nightmares. After a while, the odd nightmare turned into full-on nightmares, and every night as the second-hand struck midnight, Samuel would wake up screaming (it sounds like a horror movie, but this was reality). The nightmares continued every night for several weeks. We prayed and asked others to pray too, but they didn't stop. We did not know what to do until a pastor called André from Cape Town, South Africa, came to stay with us while visiting France.

He told us that as Lyon was considered to be the occult capital of Europe, there was a lot of bad spiritual activity going on around our neighbourhood. He believed that at that specific time when Samuel was experiencing nightmares, there was occultic practice taking place. André said that he believed Samuel had a prophetic gift, and that possibly this was the reason why he was sensitive to this activity and was affected by what was going on in the area. André took authority over the witchcraft in our neighbourhood and prayed for protection over Samuel in the name of Jesus, asking God to give him good sleep. He spoke Scripture over him too: "*I will both lie down in peace, and sleep; For you alone, O LORD, make me dwell in safety.*" *Psalm 4:8 (NKJV).* Immediately after André had prayed, the nightmares stopped and never happened again. He stayed with us for a week, affirming us in our calling and encouraging us to keep on trusting God.

After an interesting year with Samuel's teacher, we started praying for a Christian teacher to come into the school for Samuel, as we didn't want another year like that! Our pastor told us that the French way of doing things in the schools would not change and that there was no point in praying. We believe God wants people to step out of the mould and believe Him for new and greater things. We therefore continued to pray for the situation to change. After the long summer holidays were over, we went to look at the lists that had been put up outside the school gates to see who Samuel's new teacher would be for that new school year. Samuel's name was on a list under a new teacher's name that no one had heard of before.

On Samuel's first day in class with his new teacher, one of the first questions she asked him was to name his siblings. When she heard that they were all names from the Bible, she worked out somehow that we were missionaries. She asked to meet with us and told us she was a Christian and said that she had also mentioned to the headmaster that there was a missionary family in the school before she had even confirmed it with us! Samuel was very excited to see how God had answered our prayers.

We saw an enormous difference that year and finally Samuel started to really love going to school. By this stage, he was reading and writing in French and English and was achieving excellent marks. He told the teacher that he considered himself to be French - well he is, as he was born in France! That year his new Christian teacher came along with Samuel's class on a week-long school trip. We wondered how he would be able to go away as he still had a problem with controlling his bladder at night, and despite our desperate efforts, he was still wearing a nappy when he went to bed, aged seven. We discretely told his teacher who was so kind and helpful. She said that she wouldn't tell any of the students or other teachers, but would take Samuel to one side to help him put his nappy on each night, so that he could still go away on the school trip. (I can't imagine that happening now with child abuse and all the red tape - things have become so complicated!). We were so grateful for her kindness to us. Thankfully, after finally visiting doctors and a specialist at the hospital nearby, we worked out that he had no serious issues. It was simply a matter of him drinking a lot more during the day and no more drinks after returning home from school late afternoon.

Halloween At School

Ugh! Halloween! As this festival is about death rather than life, we didn't want our children to be involved in any school activities that celebrated it. Unfortunately, Deborah came home after school one day singing some dreadful song about blood curdling screams, witches and other frightening things, so we asked to have a meeting with the teacher. Deborah's teacher was on leave, so the supply teacher asked us to see the headmistress instead. Remembering the conversation that we had with our pastor about how difficult it would be to change the French schooling system, we prayed for favour with her. She was so lovely and easy to talk to, and to our surprise she said she didn't like

Halloween either. The following day we again bumped into the headmistress at school. She told us about her decision to destroy all the song books and other things to do with Halloween in the school, as she had found other fun activities for the pupils to do instead! Wow, what an answer to prayer!

An Adventurous Shopping Trip

"Courage in danger is half the battle." Plautus

One Saturday morning we all went to the large Auchan shopping centre in St Priest to do our grocery shopping. I decided before entering the shops to draw some money out from the ATM. I left Paul to look after the children just a short distance away. There were two men wearing motorbike helmets in front of the ATM; they had a trolley with a huge cardboard box in it lying sideways. They seemed to be taking a long time to draw out money, so I asked them if the dispenser was working. One answered, "Yes," and the other answered, "No!" I turned to look at Paul and he motioned to me to come quickly. He had seen from a different angle that one of the men had a screwdriver and was trying to break into the cash machine while hiding behind the cardboard box. We hurried into the shop and Paul told the security guard standing by the entrance what was going on. Immediately the camera that was facing the entrance of the building turned to face the men with their shopping trolley.

They noticed something was going on and fled. Later that day we had a phone call from the police to ask us if we could give an account of what happened. A policeman came to interview us, and one of the questions asked was if I had seen the faces of the men; I told him that I could only see their eyes. The policeman then revealed to us that both men had been wearing balaclavas under their helmets, and that was the reason why it was impossible to see their faces. The men had been chased by plain-clothes policemen when they fled and were finally caught. We were told that the robbers were armed and that the police had been trying to find them for five years! They were mafia gang members from Italy and had previously committed other crimes. It was shocking to think that I had been talking to them at the cash dispenser when they had been armed! We thanked God for protecting our family.

GAYNOR VAN DER HAGEN

The Fall Of Madame Achard

"It's Not the Years in Your Life That Count.
It's the Life in Your Years."
Abraham Lincoln

One morning I was going down the stairs outside our house into the courtyard when I heard a very strange noise that sounded a bit like a bird with a very repetitive song. It was strangely restrained, "Au Secours," "Au Secours," "Au Secours," "Au Secours." I ran back up the stairs to see where the noise was coming from, and to my horror, saw an old lady lying on her back in the garden next door calling for help. I quickly put Joshua in his playpen, locked the back door and hurried down the road around the corner to their gate. I peered over the wall and could see her lying there. I tried the gate, but it was locked, so I scrambled quickly over the top of the wall and jumped into the garden. Madame Achard told me she had fallen. I tried to help her sit up as the ground she was lying on was cold, hard concrete (I only realised afterwards that it wasn't wise to do that). She was in pain, in shock and felt cold. I knew that I couldn't help her, so I phoned for an ambulance. I then rushed up their stairs as I saw that the front door was open; she needed something warm around her urgently. I grabbed the first warm bed throw that I could find and ran back down the stairs. She wasn't happy about me taking that one, as she said it was too nice to put on the floor!! I then had to rush back up the stairs again and managed to find a very warm coat that was hanging behind the door. I tried to put it over her and around her frail body carefully to keep her warm. I had to find the spare key to open the gate so that when the ambulance came, they could come in with their stretcher. Thankfully I found the key in the hallway on the key rack close to the front door. The ambulance came quickly as the hospital was not far away, and the dear old lady was put onto a stretcher and taken away. I learnt later that she had fractured her hip, but I was so grateful I was home that morning and able to help her.

CHAPTER 17

Miracles Do Happen

"Faith sees the invisible, believes the incredible, and receives the impossible."
Corrie ten Boom

HERE IS A SHORT EXTRACT from a newsletter we sent out in December 2005, giving an update of some of the highlights of the year:

Family

Gaynor's brother and sister made a surprise visit to see her parents who were staying with us, and we were all together as a family for the first time in 12 years!

In November we celebrated our 12.5-year wedding anniversary - a great Dutch tradition. They do this because it is halfway to the 25th anniversary. We treated ourselves to an excellent Nigel Kennedy concert to celebrate the occasion.

All four of our children contracted scarlet fever and Samuel had a nasty dose of it. Deborah was the last to get it and she looked so beautiful with her rosy cheeks. Samuel is now helping his teacher with her English classes and is progressing well in French. Deborah is in her first year at primary school and is starting to read. Rebecca is in her second year at kindergarten and writes her name already and enjoys speaking French with her friends. Joshua has just celebrated his second birthday and every day he discovers new words. His favourite word now is "pie" which means "light" to him. He loves seeing all the Christmas lights in the shops when we go out. He has finally been healed from respiratory problems and we are so thankful.

Church

We continue to attend a church in St Etienne, about an hour's drive from Lyon. It is a long way to travel every Sunday, but we like being there. Gaynor recently became one of the Sunday school teachers and has been enjoying teaching a group of ten young children, and Paul has been busy putting the church website together.

In December we organised another traditional "English Carol Evening" in our home. We invited people we had met through school for mince pies, mulled wine and Christmas carols. Eight adults and Eight children came, and they loved the English and French carols that we sang. They asked for "encores" and one lady said, "It was an evening she would never forget."

We finished our Alpha course in June this year and have decided to run another one in January.

Life Is Precious - February 2006

When you arise in the morning, think of what a precious privilege it is to be alive - to breathe, to think, to enjoy, to love.
Marcus Aurelius

My mother in Zimbabwe had been suffering from ill-health for a while. We received a call from my dad to say that she had been admitted to hospital and was in intensive care as her condition had deteriorated. It was so difficult being far away from them, and especially during that time. We were grateful that we could still pray. On Saturday 11th of February, I had been praying for her and felt God remind me of the following Bible verse:

"This is what the Sovereign Lord says to these bones:
I will make breath enter you, and you will come to life."
Ezekiel 37:5 (NIV)

I phoned my dad and asked him to read this verse to my mom to encourage her, as she was struggling to breathe. Mom wrote it in her Bible and shared it with the doctor looking after her who was a Christian. He decided that because of the Bible verse he had just read, he would prescribe the strongest antibiotic possible to fight all types of lung infections (not knowing if a lung infection was the cause of the illness or not). As the economic situation in Zimbabwe was so bad, they were unable to buy the medication that she so desperately needed (Montelukast), which was to help with asthma and difficulty in breathing. My dad called asking if we could get the medication sent to Zimbabwe as urgently as possible. The problem was that the doctor's surgery in Harare had been broken into and his computer had been stolen. There was therefore no way that he could send us a prescription by email. The only solution I had was to speak to our French pharmacist and beg them to sell me the medication over the counter without a prescription.

Thankfully it was not the first time they had dealt with my mother, as she had been ill in France once before while on holiday. Much to my relief, they agreed to give me the medication for her. I then had to book a courier to fly it to Zimbabwe. The choice was to use either FedEx or DHL. It was Saturday and FedEx said they could only deliver the medication by Wednesday the following week, and DHL said they could only deliver it by Thursday. My mom needed the medication by Monday at the latest, and we had no means of being able to do that. We decided to go with FedEx, as their service would arrive one day earlier.

We then prayed again for a miracle that somehow, God would do something to get it there by Monday. We tracked it online to see where it was throughout the day, and then we received this message, "Arrived, Harare, 16:45, Monday 13 February 2006." Monday??? God had done something amazing which both courier services had said was impossible. The following day after my mother had started to take the antibiotic treatment, she was able to sit up in bed with her legs stretched out in front of her. She hadn't been able to do that for a long time because of the shortness of breath. Her legs were so swollen that they looked like tree trunks; they needed to be kept up so that the fluid could start to drain. She started to regain her strength and soon was allowed home. We praised God for healing her.

Filling In The Gap

> *"A mind that is stretched by a new experience can never go back to its old dimensions."*
> Oliver Wendell Holmes, Jr.

It had already been one year since we started attending the church in St Etienne. We had come to the realisation that we had to stop what we had been trying to do on our own in Lyon. However, living far away from the church in St Etienne did not allow us to be fully involved there, and we realised that at some point it would come to an end as we could not keep on driving two hours there and back every Sunday. We had given ourselves that year to seek God's leading and to decide what to do next. While involved in that church, I saw that there was a need for a Sunday school teacher for children between the ages of three and eight years old. I didn't feel that I was particularly gifted in that area, but knew that our children and other children needed someone to teach them. Each week I prepared a lesson for the children and organised games and colouring activities. From the USA we ordered beautifully illustrated story books that used realistic pictures to tell Bible stories. The children loved them, and I started to enjoy it too, although it was difficult teaching them in French.

On Mother's Day one Sunday, I decided to teach the children about love. I baked a huge quantity of heart biscuits at home, iced and decorated them with miniature pink and red hearts, so that the children could hand them out to their parents in the congregation as a love gift. I taught the children a song to sing about the love of Jesus and they sang it to their parents at the front of the church. I could see how much the parents enjoyed watching their children sing, and how the children enjoyed giving out the biscuits to their parents afterwards.

When we returned home after the service, I felt that God was pleased with what I had done. I walked into the kitchen and saw something shining on the floor. It was a gold heart pendant from a necklace. Nobody had been to our house that week, and I didn't own one. I still to this day don't know where it came from, but it didn't seem like a coincidence. I believe God had sent an angel to bring it to me to say thank you. I still have it and it is a wonderful reminder of what happened that day.

The gold heart pendant

Trouble In The Cities....

In October and November 2005, a series of riots occurred in the suburbs of Paris and other French cities, including Lyon. This involved the burning of cars and public buildings at night. The unrest started on the 27th of October in Paris where police were investigating a reported break-in at a building site; a group of local youths scattered to avoid interrogation. Three of them hid in a power-station where two died from electrocution, resulting in a power blackout. (It was not established whether police had suspected these individuals, or if it was a different group wanted on separate charges). The incident ignited rising tensions about youth unemployment and police harassment in the poorer housing estates, and three weeks of rioting followed throughout France. The riots resulted in three deaths of non-rioters and many police injuries, and nearly 3,000 arrests were made.

Troublemakers unfortunately came very close to our home, and one of the cars behind our back yard was set alight and choking black smoke belched out. The fire was soon out of control, and the car next to it also caught fire. In the middle of the night, residents from a small apartment block opposite our house were evacuated. The gas pipe next to the cars could have melted from the extreme heat, and there was a serious risk of a gas explosion. Our house was closer to the gas pipe than the apartment block. It was surprising that we weren't evacuated as well, as we could have been seriously injured if an explosion had taken place. We were grateful that we were able to keep on sleeping and to stay warm inside, instead of standing at a distance on the pavement all night!

What's Your Name?

"A good name is to be chosen rather than great riches,
loving favour rather than silver and gold."
Proverbs 22:1 (NKJV)

One Sunday just before Christmas, I decided to teach the children at church about the birth of Jesus. One of the young teenagers from another Sunday school class, asked me if it was possible for her to come and help me with the younger children. She was a very unhappy child and did not fit in well with her peers. She decided to help me on a regular basis, and I was glad that she had found a place where she felt safe and could relax. The lesson I had prepared for that day was about the meaning of Jesus's name (Saviour). To make it more interesting, I thought that the children might like to find out the meaning of their own names. I brought in a couple of baby name books so that I could look up their names. I was surprised, as only a few of the children knew what their names meant. Most of their names had lovely meanings; some were names of places or flowers.

Unfortunately, my lovely teenage helper didn't look very happy when I started talking about the meaning of our names. When it was her turn to talk about her name, she told me that she already knew what her name meant - *pain*. It was an awkward moment and I wondered how I would deal with it. Suddenly I had an idea to ask her if she had a second name. "Yes, Nadia," she replied. I hurriedly looked up the meaning, desperate for something positive – "*hope*," I said. Her second name meant HOPE! Wow! I was able to tell her that Jesus had taken her *pain and* had replaced it with HOPE - hope for her future. Her face transformed from that of someone who had been really struggling with life, to someone who was peaceful and content! From that moment on, I saw such a positive transformation in that precious girl's life that I was glad I had made the effort to teach the children even though I didn't think I was gifted to do it. I had helped her have a different outlook on life.

In Transit - August 2006

Hewlett-Packard had announced that 20% of its employees, and 50% of the people at Paul's site would be made redundant. Paul wasn't sure about his position but thought it would be wise to search for IT jobs in Lyon just in case. He sent out over 50 job applications and had a handful of interviews, but no job offers. We began to wonder whether we would be able to continue to stay in Lyon should his job come to an end. We often talked about how we believed we were meant to stay there for the rest of our lives. We also discussed all our efforts to start a church and how we had been reaching out to those in our community. Our hearts were 100% engaged in what we had been trying to achieve, but we sadly hadn't seen much fruit. We had tried to run the church by ourselves as unfortunately, no one was prepared to take a big step of faith to help us. We had taken a year out to see what God would do, and we had gained some valuable experience in the church in St Etienne. However, we knew the reality was that we needed work to support us financially to continue to stay in Lyon. We felt very discouraged and cried a lot. We were comforted knowing that every tear we cried was important to God.

"You keep track of all my sorrows. You have collected all my tears in your bottle. You have recorded each one in your book."
Psalm 56:8 (NLT)

CHAPTER 18

On The Move Again

"Never worry about numbers. Help one person at a time, and always start with the person nearest you."
Mother Teresa

ONE DAY while Paul was praying, he felt God tell him that He was going to provide financially for our family through other means, and that he would no longer be working for Hewlett-Packard. There didn't seem to be any suitable jobs for Paul in Lyon, so he decided to widen his job search. He found out that in Sophia-Antipolis (France's Silicon Valley near Nice in the South of France), there were many international IT companies looking to recruit people with his profile. He sent a few application letters, and recruitment agencies immediately started to call him to arrange interviews. A week later he was invited to fly to Nice and was offered a job as a Systems Administrator at IBM. The speed at which all these things happened took us by surprise. We had not expected this door to open and only had a short time to decide whether we should accept it and leave Lyon for good or not.

Paul's job interview coincided with a short holiday that we had planned two months previously. Our holiday apartment was near St Tropez, not too far from where IBM was located (I don't believe this was a coincidence). While we were on holiday, we decided to visit Nice and its region to see if we felt it was right to move there. As the Cote d'Azur is very popular with tourists and people retiring, property prices are high. Before accepting the offer, we needed to find out if we could afford to live there. (We realise now that regardless of whether the cost of living is high or not, if God calls us, He will provide and we must learn to trust Him). We tried to understand why God would be sending us there, as we felt we had not finished our work in Lyon. Nevertheless, we believe that God orders our steps and that He opens and closes doors, but we didn't understand why He would be sending us to the French Riviera.

"The steps of a good man are ordered by the Lord, and He delights in his way." Psalm 37:23 (NKJV).

This Bible verse was reassuring, although we continued to hope that the doors to Nice would close (we understand now that we had done what God had asked us to do in Lyon, and that we had sown seeds and toiled the land).

"This is the meaning of the parable: The seed is God's word."
Luke 8:11 (NLT)

It was very hard for us to leave Lyon as in some ways we felt we had failed. We had lived there for ten years and had talked to many people about God. We had worked very hard to help people but had only seen one person give their life to God and had baptised one other. The following Bible verse reassured us that our labour was not in vain:

"For in this the saying is true: 'One sows and another reaps.'
I sent you to reap that for which you have not laboured; others
have laboured, and you have entered into their labours."
John 4:37-38 (NKJV)

It was up to God to water the seeds that we had sown, and to bring them to fruition in His timing. Now back to our holiday… During our visit to Nice, we decided to visit a church in the area which we had vaguely heard about. Even though Paul's job offer was compelling, the most important focus for us was to find a church where we could be involved and use our gifts, should we decide to move. The moment we arrived at the church, we felt at home. We were very warmly welcomed, and the leaders offered to help us settle into the region (we later found out that they had been praying for families to join them and help them with their different activities and projects.). The services were bilingual (English and French), with a congregation of around 200 people. The church ran a soup kitchen/coffee bar, a charity shop and reached out to needy people in the area. It had also been running Alpha courses and needed people to help organise further courses. They wanted to provide training for the unemployed and it looked like there would be many opportunities for us to help out.

Paul was invited to speak at their Wednesday evening meetings, and I was asked to help with the Sunday school even before we had arrived! After we concluded that God was leading us, Paul accepted the job at IBM and resigned from Hewlett-Packard. He started his new job mid-June that year and enjoyed the change of environment and working with his new colleagues. During the week he stayed in an apartment, a stone's throw from the beach, and travelled home by train every weekend. The rest of our family were not able to leave Lyon immediately. We wanted our children to finish their school term and we also had renovation work scheduled for the end of June (it had been planned the previous year). I needed to do some work in the attic, kitchen and lounge and had all our belongings to pack too. Packing the children's things was tough. They would notice that a particular toy was no longer around and ask for it, or they would see me packing one of them away and start crying, asking to have it back. They couldn't understand that they would see everything again once we had arrived in our new home. I had to put up with a lot of tears which was hard for me to bear on my own!

From April that year, when we had made the decision to move, we worked non-stop on our house - often until midnight or later, desperately trying to complete the work by the end of July. I was so busy, not only looking after our four kids, but also preparing for the move, dealing with builders, as well as painting and decorating. With temperatures of around 38 degrees Celsius and the windows closed because of the building work, I was stretched to the limit. Our children coped very well with the changes considering the circumstances and the heat.

Even though this was certainly the most testing time we had experienced in ten years, we could see that the move was the right thing to do, and we had peace to leave Lyon behind us. We realised that since our arrival in Lyon, we hadn't really settled. We often felt lonely and isolated, and only had a few close friends. We had seen God provide supernaturally for us there and knew He would continue to do so.

Our most urgent need was to find a house to rent, however, we discovered that we would be arriving at the wrong time of the year – August, which brought many tourists to that region and there were only a few places available to rent long-term. Most apartments were rented out to tourists on a weekly basis, and rental prices for houses were way above our budget.

After looking for months, we finally found a small three-bedroom house (through someone we had met at church), in a picturesque Provencal village, called Le Rouret. We decided to move there at the beginning of August, as the start of the new school year was September.

We were finally able to pack a small rental van with the essential things (our beds and clothes) that we would need for our first few months. A removal company brought the rest of our belongings a few months later. The children came in the car with me, and we followed closely behind Paul as he drove the van.

Ready to leave Lyon

CHAPTER 19

Arriving In The South Of France

"Every end is a new beginning."
Unknown

AFTER A FIVE-HOUR JOURNEY we finally arrived in Le Rouret. The house we had rented was very old. It had cold tiled flooring, was badly insulated and the walls were damp with bubbles coming out of the paint where the humidity couldn't escape (it was tempting to push them in to see if any water would ooze out). Like most houses in France, it had shutters. There were also shutters that closed in front of the French doors - possibly to help keep out the cold, or for added security. It was strange that the French doors didn't have any keys, so we were unable to lock them. The shutters had ill-fitting hinges and handles, and it didn't feel very safe leaving our belongings in the house. We approached the agents and asked them to supply keys, but they said they didn't have any and that there had never been any issues with the house. They told us that they would not do anything to improve it, and we were thankful that we weren't going to stay there too long.

Our first home for three months in Le Rouret

As Paul was already working when we arrived, we didn't have much to do, except unpack boxes, so I decided to take the children to the beach for the day. I discussed with Paul the night before where I should take them, and he told me not to go to Cannes as it would be too difficult keeping an eye on all four of them by myself (aged nine, seven, five and three). The following morning, I took out the GPS and looked up where the nearest beaches were. There were many to choose from and it didn't mean anything to me as I didn't know the area. I therefore thought it would be safer to select the beach that was the closest. The drive was lovely but nearing our destination, the traffic started getting very busy and then I saw, "Welcome to Cannes!" We had arrived at the very beach we had been trying to avoid. I decided to go with the flow and parked the car in the nearest underground car park. We clambered out of the car grabbing our towels, goggles, armbands, sun cream and bottles of water and walked a short way through the crowd until we found a place to put our belongings down on the beach.

I explained all the golden rules to the children, covered them from head to toe with sun cream (which took forever) and then sat on my beach towel to guard all our belongings. It was busy on the beach, and I was conscious that the current was dragging our children further and further to the right of where I was sitting.

After a short while, Joshua decided he had had enough of playing in the sea and wanted to make sandcastles. The girls wanted to continue swimming with their armbands on, and Samuel wanted to look for fish with his swimming goggles. There were several children looking for fish using their goggles and bobbing up and down. It was difficult to know which children were mine. Feeling very nervous, I left my belongings and went to find them. The number of children on the beach had increased and it became too tricky for me to keep my eyes on them all doing different things. With four very disappointed children, I reassured them that we would return to the beach again, but insisted that Daddy would have to be there as well. I had never felt so relieved to have all our precious children back in the car, as I was then!

As I mentioned, our new accommodation wasn't great, and unfortunately when it turned cold, we started having problems with the boiler. This meant we had no hot water for several days. This was very challenging as you can imagine with four young children. I tried to get the agent to ask the owner to replace the old boiler, but she wasn't very motivated (that's putting it kindly!). It broke down seven times every few days and she would send her handyman to try and repair it. Someone I met gave me the name of the owner and her home address, so I boldly went to her gate and rang the bell. She lived at a beautiful villa not far from the centre of the village. The lady, who was perhaps in her 70s, came hesitantly to the gate, screwing her eyes up tightly to see if she recognised me. "Are you the lady who owns the old house in Chemin des Princes," I asked? "It depends," she replied!!! I told her that we had four young children and were struggling to keep warm, and that boiling pots of water on the stove to give my children a bath every evening was not only frustrating, but extremely inconvenient. To my surprise, she showed no compassion at all and refused to change the boiler. We were so glad that we didn't have to stay in that house for long. Le Rouret was half an hour from Nice, 25 minutes from our new church and 10 km from the beach. Over a period of months, we actively looked to buy a house and prayed for a home large enough for our family; we also hoped to have separate accommodation to receive relatives and friends. Joshua (two and a half years old) prayed that the house would have a swimming pool, "House, swimming pool, amen." Due to the very warm climate in the summer, it really is a necessity! Just before leaving Lyon, we had found a house for sale on the Internet that interested us. Shortly afterwards, we noticed that it was no longer advertised on the website. When we arrived in our new church, we spoke to a lady about it and showed her the advert we had saved from a magazine, thinking it had been sold.

She laughed and said she knew exactly where the house was - it was her neighbour's! Sadly, she explained that her neighbours were getting a divorce and that they had taken the house off the market, as the wife wanted to see if she would be able to afford to continue to live there with her children. We asked our friend to keep us informed if her neighbour changed her mind, and if possible, give us the first option to buy it.

Le Rouret, our village with Gréolières in the background

After visiting quite a few houses, the house that we were initially interested in came back on the market. It was exactly what we had been looking for. It had four bedrooms, an office, lounge and dining room, a pool and a fully equipped guest cottage with two bedrooms. Best of all, we didn't need to do any work on it! As the houses in the region were so expensive, this one seemed the only possible option, as we could use the separate guest house as a "gîte" (holiday home) to rent out. This would bring in the necessary income to pay for the mortgage. We had agreed on the sale price with the owners and had set a date to sign the initial sales agreement with the solicitors. Two days before signing, we received a phone call from the owner to say that she had changed her mind and would no longer be selling the house to us. She had found someone else who was prepared to pay 30,000 euros more. We asked ourselves if they really had found a buyer who was prepared to pay more, or if they were trying to get more money out of us. We couldn't believe that they would go back on their word. We therefore had to find another 30,000 euros, which we didn't have, if we wanted to buy the house! After contacting our bank, they agreed to include the 30,000 euros in our mortgages and to give us a bridging loan on the house that we were selling in Lyon. This meant that we would have two mortgages to pay, one for the "gîte", and one for the other part of the house that we would live in. That was stressful! At the end of July, Paul signed the initial sales agreement, and we were given the keys in November 2006.

The lady we bought the house from had to stay in our "gîte" for a further two weeks until she was able to move into her accommodation. What we didn't realise was that she had been dishonest about the swimming pool and hadn't told us that the skimmers had a bad leak. Each time we had visited the house before buying it, she had topped up the pool to make it look like it was functioning properly. As we had to borrow more money to buy the house, we were unable to pay to have the pool repaired.

This meant that the skimmers could never be used, and I had to clean the pool daily to take out the leaves and other things that floated in it. It was a lot of work, but Joshua's prayers had been answered and we were thankful to still be able to use the pool. Unfortunately, our house in Lyon didn't sell quickly as the estate agent in Lyon had incorrectly advised us on the value of our property. It took one and a half years to sell, which put us in an extremely stressful situation financially.

Flame Lily Lodge

*"You don't stop laughing when you grow old,
you grow old when you stop laughing."*
George Bernard Shaw

On our first day in our new home, our children excitedly took out their new toys that they had been given by a church in Sacramento, California. They had been sent some fantastic looking dinosaurs that made realistic noises when you squeezed them. They spent the whole day playing outside and hiding their toys among the bushes to make it look like a scene from Jurassic Park. When it was time to come in for dinner, they asked me if they could leave their toys outside so that they could play with them again the following day. The next morning while the children were still sleeping, I went outside to discover my new garden. I was expecting to hear birds, but there was a very strange squawking and indescribable wailing noise instead. I followed the noises to see where they came from. To my horror, I came across chewed up bits of dinosaur strewn all over the place. Some of them decapitated and were making terrible noises. Some were covered in saliva, and I realised that the St Bernard dogs we had seen in our neighbour's garden the previous day had escaped and had destroyed our children's toys. I quickly went to get one of the removal boxes from inside the house. I filled it with all the chewed-up pieces of toys and hid them out of sight. I went to tell Paul and he was very unhappy to say the least! When our children finally came outside to play, the look on their faces said it all! Shock, horror, disappointment, tears - and we couldn't show them what their dinosaurs looked like as it would have been too much for them to bear. There was only one dinosaur left out of the 12; it had canine teeth marks on it but could still be played with.

We decided to go and visit our neighbour a few days after that when he returned from work. We took the removal box of chewed up dinosaurs that we had gathered so that we could show him what his dogs had done. We mentioned that they were special gifts our children had received from friends in the USA. We could not believe his response. He laughed almost until his stomach hurt, and then he told us to go back to America, and he meant it! The two dogs became a huge problem for us because they kept escaping from their garden and doing their business on our property. Our children, however, were delighted to have an opportunity to play with them whenever they saw them.

Our neighbour's dog was pregnant and eventually gave birth to seven puppies. We had the last laugh as they were obliged to repair the fence to keep them all in - and you can imagine the amount of dog mess they had to clean up every day, with two adult dogs and all those puppies!

"A day without flowers is like a heart without memories."
Carolyn Ericson

Our garden had seven olive trees, oleander hedges in deep pink, pale pink and white. We also had a lemon tree, a walnut tree, two cherry trees, a Seville orange tree, several palm trees, cacti and beautiful flowers and shrubs. Unfortunately, some of us were allergic to the cherry and olive tree flowers. One flower that had the strongest scent in our garden and attracted several bees in the summer was the flowering ivy hedge. One day Samuel went outside to play with his ball; the sun was shining on the ivy blossom causing the flowers to omit a very strong odour. As he continued to play close by, he suddenly had an asthma attack. His throat started swelling up and he fell onto his knees struggling to breathe. Thankfully I saw it happening and I ran to him and felt led to speak out in a loud voice, commanding asthma to leave his body. I said, "Asthma, you are to leave his body and never come back again." I had a Ventolin inhaler in my handbag and encouraged Samuel to breathe out as much as possible and then to breathe the medication in slowly. It rapidly had an effect, helping him to regain his breath. I prayed over him immediately against any fear, but also against the belief that he might have developed asthma. I also prayed that he would never have another asthma attack again. I was grateful the Ventolin had helped him, knowing that God can heal through medication but also through prayer. (I am thankful to say that 15 years later he is still free from asthma and has never had symptoms like that ever again).

Once we were finally settled, we began to prepare our "gîte" (holiday home) so that we could rent it out as soon as possible. We chose the name, "Flame Lily Lodge" which we named after the national flower of Zimbabwe. The kitchen was painted in deep oranges and yellows which really suited the name. A representative from "Gîte de France" registered it as a three-star "gîte". We found an excellent website called "AngloInfo" that expats used to sell their belongings, or to give them away when they would relocate. We managed to find many free things in excellent condition to furnish it and we had friends who worked on the superyachts in Monaco who gave us free linen. Their superyacht was supplied with new luxury linen yearly, so that was very helpful. We needed to buy two extra single beds and had seen an advert on "AngloInfo" for a second-hand good quality bed and arranged to have a look at it. The lady was very friendly and asked us what we did for a

Flame Lily Lodge

living. Paul talked about his work in IT, and she then asked him to help her upload some photos from her camera to her computer. He spent some time trying to work it out, but it turned out not to be as simple as he had thought. We left and promised to do some research before returning the following day to pick up the bed. She was so happy that Paul was able to eventually help her access her photos on her computer that she refused payment for the bed. She visited us a few weeks later to give us another bed, a hand painted mirror, a beautiful wrought iron bookcase with oak shelving and some skiing clothes, as they were leaving the country. Our "gîte" was very successful and we had many bookings throughout the summer months. Some tourists came from Ireland, Zimbabwe, Germany, the UK and Quebec to name a few. The only problem with taking bookings in the summer meant that we could never go away during that time, as that was the most profitable period and it enabled us to pay our mortgages. When the summer months came to an end, we rented "Flame Lily Lodge" out on a six-month short-term lease.

Institute Fénelon - Grasse

"Work hard, be kind and amazing things will happen."
Conan O'Brien

Our financial struggles meant that when Samuel and Deborah moved from their primary school in Le Rouret to their secondary school, "Fénelon International College" in Grasse, that we were unable to pay for them to eat lunch in the canteen. The school had strict rules; if pupils were not paying to eat in the canteen, they were to go home to eat their lunch and were not allowed to bring packed lunches to school. The canteen was expensive for us (six euros a meal), and it was one of the ways the school made their money. We lived too far from the college for our children to be able to come home for lunch, so they were told to eat their sandwiches in between the two school gates. They had to wait outside for half an hour until the school bell rang, which was a sign that the students had finished eating in the canteen and were ready to return to class. Sometimes it would rain very hard, or it was cold or possibly snowing and they would have to wait outside shivering. I remember sitting at home feeling guilty because my children were outside in the cold and I was inside, dry and warm.

Say What?

After two months of working at IBM, Paul came home to tell me that he had worked his last day there. I couldn't believe it. We had made the move all the way from Lyon to the South of France for that job and it was already over. It was so scary for us as we had a lot of debt to pay. We had three mortgages - one for our house, one for the "gîte" and the bridging loan for the house in Lyon that was not yet sold, and six mouths to feed!! We prayed earnestly asking God to help. Thankfully, Paul had kept some contact details from colleagues he had been working with and asked them to help him look for possible vacancies.

Soon afterwards he applied for another job at IBM that he didn't have the skills for. He tried to prepare for the interview but had no idea how to. His interview lasted five minutes. The hiring manager, knowing that

Paul had previously worked for IBM, asked him if he was bilingual, if he had a wife and how many children he had. That was the interview! He never once asked him if he had any experience in that field, and thankfully he didn't! Paul was offered the job and just about coped from there on. Thankfully some colleagues were patient enough to teach him and helped him adapt and develop in that area.

CHAPTER 20

A Time For Everything

*"Tranquillity is a Choice. So is Anxiety.
The entire world around us may be in
turmoil. But if we want to be Peaceful
within, WE CAN."*
Unknown

2007: WE WERE SETTLED in our new home,
although our financial situation was always in the back
of our minds. We desperately needed people to make
reservations for our "gîte" which would help us to keep
our heads above water. Thankfully we were living in a
holiday destination and could go for trips to the sea or
have fun in the river nearby. Doing these things with
our children didn't cost much. One Sunday after
church, we decided to take the children to visit an

amusement park not far from where we lived so that they could run around and have some fun. It was called "Ludiparc" in La Colle sur Loup, a beautiful, natural environment with oak, olive and pine trees and a river with crystal clear water.

There was a trampoline and a zip line (which I call a foefie slide) and some other climbing frames. Samuel decided to run off and have a go on the zip line. I went after him, and Paul stayed to watch the others on the trampoline. Samuel tried to climb onto it without waiting for me to hold it and it started to move without him. He fell back and hit his head so hard on the ground that I could hear it. I shouted to Paul, and he grabbed the others off the trampoline and came running. Samuel lay there dazed; he could feel pins and needles in his legs - we feared the worst but prayed he would be alright. We took him carefully to the car and brought him home to lie down. In hindsight, we should have called for an ambulance. Shortly afterwards, he started vomiting and that was when we made the decision to take him to the accident and emergency department at the hospital. Samuel was x-rayed and the result was that he had very bad whiplash and was asked to wear a cervical collar for several weeks. Thankfully there was no long-lasting injury, and we were only too aware what a miracle that was!

To add to that, Rebecca had been suffering from a very bad tight chest and bronchitis and I had made an appointment for her to see the doctor. Deborah had also been complaining about a sore belly for some time; she had a tender area just above her belt, but we didn't think it was anything to worry about, and I had forgotten about it as she hardly mentioned it. A couple of weeks after Samuel's accident, I fetched the children from school and brought them into the doctor's room with me so that Rebecca could be seen. I suddenly remembered Deborah's tummy and thought I should ask the doctor about it. She examined her carefully, pressing gently around the area where it had been painful. "Deborah has an umbilical hernia that needs urgent attention," she said. The doctor called the hospital to make an appointment, and the following day we went to "L'Archet", a hospital in Nice. The specialist took one look at her and said, "I'm scheduling her in for emergency surgery tomorrow (the 13th of July)." The umbilical hernia risked erupting and she told us it could be life-threatening! The following morning, I dropped the other children off at our pastor's house as Paul had to go to work and then drove on to the hospital with Deborah. I was given several forms to complete and was so grateful that by this stage my French had improved considerably, and I was able to understand most of the questions that the doctor asked me. Deborah had key-hole surgery and the operation was a success.

The surgeon told me after the operation that it was incredible that Deborah had the surgery when she did, as she was scheduled to go on a three-week holiday the following day and there would not have been anyone qualified to deal with that type of emergency! God was looking after us. Deborah was given a light meal after her surgery, and as she had fasted from dinner and breakfast, she was glad to be able to eat something again. We were allowed to leave later that day to fetch the others from our pastor's house

When I arrived the gates were open, which was unusual, but I knew that they would be expecting us, so I presumed that they had left them open on purpose. I was about to drive up their steep driveway when I noticed a huge green snake lying right across it. It was almost the width of their driveway in length, and at least 10 cm wide, if not more. I suddenly thought that as their gate was always closed, their son had played a trick on us and had put his huge toy snake there to scare me. I didn't want to damage it, so I put the handbrake on and climbed out of the car to move it out of the way. The snake suddenly came to life, and then as if doing a slalom, he thankfully slithered quickly away from me into the trees. I held back a scream. I have never seen such a huge snake in my life so close! I would have expected this in Africa, but certainly not in the South of France! It felt like my heart had stopped for a moment. I ran back to the car, drove up the hill and then jumped out of the car and hurriedly ran inside to tell our friends all about the snake. Thankfully, their three little dogs were all safe. The hunt was now on to find the snake...

Making Pancakes

I had been having burning pain in my breasts for a while and after a visit to my GP, was sent to have some mammograms done. The results showed that I had calcifications that were dense, and they looked ominous. Two weeks after Deborah's surgery, I was scheduled for a series of biopsies. It was a challenge to remain positive. This was the third hospital we were visiting in a matter of weeks!

We chose not to tell the children but asked some close friends to pray with us. I had three biopsies done and was in a lot of pain afterwards. I was told that the results would come in the post. Some nights before going to sleep, Paul and I would cry together, just wondering what the future would hold. It took a few weeks for the results to come back. During that time of waiting, Paul had given me a Bible verse which I spoke out loud over myself every day: "*I shall not die, but live, and declare the works of the Lord.*" Psalm 118:17 (KJV). It was a huge comfort to me.

The letter finally came, and I couldn't open it fast enough. I skimmed the page trying to understand all the French but then my eye caught one word – "bénin" – benign, no cancer! I praised God for my life!

A Trip To The Circus

> *"When A Dog Bites a Man that is not news,*
> *but when a man bites a dog that is news."*
> *Charles Anderson Dana*

Every summer, Valbonne (a beautiful old town near Nice), hosted one of France's most famous travelling circuses, Cirque Arlette Gruss. Tickets to go to the circus were expensive, but one could go in the afternoons and buy cheap tickets to see all the animals before the shows. They had tigers (the most beautiful to see was the white tiger), horses, camels, lions, elephants, zebras and wallabies, to name a few. It was a huge circus that brought people from all over the world. Our children loved to go and see the animals every year; we did have the privilege of seeing a show once too. Coming from Zimbabwe, I hate seeing animals in captivity, however, these were well looked after. On one occasion, when we had finished visiting the animals, we started to walk towards the car park. Rebecca was trailing behind us. We had taken a different route back via the caravans that the circus performers lived in. Suddenly, I heard a ferocious dog barking and turned to see a pit bull gnashing his teeth and charging after her. He was very close to biting her when without even thinking, I yelled out pointing at the dog, "In the name of Jesus, go!!" I was surprised that I did that as I had never done anything like that before. To my amazement, the dog immediately turned around and started yelping as if I had hurt him! He put his tale between his legs and went running off, turning his head awkwardly several times to see if we were going to follow him. I picked up Rebecca and carried her, hurrying back to the car to catch up with the others. My heart was pounding, and I was stunned and in awe at what had just happened. The name of Jesus is so powerful, and that day, I learnt that when we speak the name of Jesus when we are in a dangerous situation, He answers.

"Call to Me, and I will answer you, and show you great and mighty things, which you do not know." Jeremiah 33:3 (NKJV)

9 "Therefore, God elevated him to the place of highest honor and gave him the name above all other names, 10that at the name of Jesus every knee should bow, in heaven and on earth and under the earth, 11and every tongue declare that Jesus Christ is Lord, to the glory of God the Father." Philippians 2:9-11 (NLT)

Parlez-vous Anglais? (Do you speak English?)

"One thing I can say about the French language is that no one in the world loves their language as much as they do. It doesn't matter if you're close - it still sounds terrible to their ears."
Mads Mikkelsen

I love that quote; it's funny and so true! French really is such a beautiful language. Although we had been in France for several years, I still had a very strong accent, and I am sure wound up a few people with my grammatical errors and poor pronunciation. Funnily enough, our children had started to experience this the other way around. It was obvious to them that their teachers were struggling to teach English to their pupils, and it made me laugh when they told me how their English lessons went, and how their teachers taught the pronunciation of certain words.

One word I remember very clearly was "chocolate". "Shock - o- late." "Shockolate." They did their best, but the English lessons were a waste of time, so I decided to offer some help. I approached the teacher in Joshua's class and mentioned that if the school was interested, I would be happy to do some English conversation classes with the students. I was also willing to do it without pay. The school told me regrettably that as I didn't have a diploma to teach English, I was not allowed to do it. It was ridiculous to think that even though I was offering free help and was a native speaker, a diploma would be the requirement. Oh well, you couldn't say I hadn't tried ☺.

CHAPTER 21

Church Life In The South Of France

"Church is not an organisation you join;
It is a family where you belong,
a home where you are loved and
a place where you find healing."
Nicky Gumbel

IT WAS GREAT to be in a church of approximately 200 people (including children). The pastor was American, and the sermons were preached in English and translated into French. Paul and I helped with the Alpha courses which were run up to five times a year. Paul led one of the groups and I helped with the catering. The courses were very popular; I remember making 100 doughnuts once for one of the sessions. I was also involved in the worship team at church and enjoyed playing my

The doughnuts I had made for the the Alpha Course

violin and singing. Paul and I taught the 11-14-year-olds group once a month and thoroughly enjoyed the challenge. It was amazing how much time it took to prepare for those Sundays. We had to be ready for whatever questions were thrown at us, and some of the children made it difficult for us on purpose. We organised fun games and quizzes and found that teaching this wonderful group of children helped our faith grow. We even did a session with them on marriage, obviously adapted to their age group, but were surprised that most of their parents hadn't taught them that a Christian should not marry an unbeliever.

"Do not be unequally yoked together with unbelievers.
For what fellowship has righteousness with lawlessness?
And what communion has light with darkness?"
2 Corinthians 6:14 (NKJV).

We knew it was vital that these young children were taught the Word of God as they are the next generation of leaders. In that group, there were several children that came from broken homes. Seeing how their lives had been affected by that, we felt that our main calling was to see marriages restored and existing marriages revived and thriving. We therefore started to help couples in the church, and after three years, were recognised by the church as leaders of the Marriage Ministry. We ran several marriage preparation courses and marriage courses in our home. I prepared and served meals for couples, providing a relaxed and romantic setting where they could discuss privately. The funniest course, and the most helpful we felt was, "Laugh Your Way to a Better Marriage" by Pastor Mark Gungor. "By using his unique blend of humour and tell-it-like-it-is honesty, Mark Gungor helps couples get along and have fun doing it."

Paul and I also initiated the potluck lunches at our church. Once a month we invited the church to make their favourite salads, main courses and desserts and we would eat together. It was the fellowship that we shared together as brothers and sisters in Christ that was so special. It was an event that everyone looked forward to. We ran these lunches for several years, coordinating everything and making sure there would be enough food for everyone attending. Writing about this reminds me about what my pastor says regarding how long one should serve in a particular ministry. He wisely suggests that at the end of each year, we should ask God if we are meant to continue serving in that ministry, or if we should let someone else do it instead and serve in another area. I was aware that my enthusiasm in running the potluck ministry was running out. People would forget to bring food, or they would bring things to share that would be less than they would have eaten had they stayed home. One family of five arrived one Sunday with only a bag of oranges and I think that was the final straw for me! It was then that I realised my gift or anointing to run the potluck lunch had worn off☺. Thankfully another lady in the church was able to take over, but this time, she ran it by buying the food herself and cooking it all onsite. People then paid to eat lunch at church. This was a different way of running it and unfortunately, less people stayed to eat together.

"Chapeau" (Congratulations)

"Education is the most powerful weapon which you can use to change the world." Nelson Mandela

After working for IBM for just over two years, Paul worked for a further two companies and was then offered a sponsorship to do a Master's degree in International Business and was accepted to join the course in the final year of the degree. The amazing thing about being accepted on the course, was that the French government paid not only for his tuition fees, but also paid him 90% of his previous salary!

Paul did really well in his exams and the graduation ceremony was to be held in Paris. As we were going to stay there just for one night, we didn't need to check in a suitcase on the flight. We put our hand luggage on the conveyor belt and the X-ray machine beeped, and Paul was called over. He had forgotten about his shaving cream and so it was thrown in the bin. The airport baggage handler continued to check through his belongings and found a bottle of aftershave which I had given him for his birthday just a few days earlier. It was expensive, and I couldn't just watch him throw it into the bin as well. I explained that it was a birthday gift, and that I had only just bought it for him. I begged him not to throw it away. Looking very solemn, he told us that he wasn't allowed to let any bottles of liquid through that exceeded 100ml. He then immediately put his finger to his lips and said, "shhh" and discreetly put it back into the bag, zipped it up and wished us a good flight!

I was so proud to be able to take photos of Paul in his mortar board (graduation cap) and gown. On returning to the airport the following day, I suddenly remembered the bottle of aftershave and wondered what would happen. We thought about paying for his hand luggage to go in the hold, but we couldn't pay any extra, so we prayed and asked God for favour again. Paul put his bag on the conveyor belt and just before it went through, I told the official that his X-ray machine was going to beep. He looked surprised. He called us aside and before he opened the hand luggage, I explained to him what had happened the previous day. He opened the zip and looked inside to see the aftershave. He shook his head sorrowfully and told us that regrettably he was not allowed to let us through the gate with anything that was over 100ml. He then quickly put it back in the bag, winked and said, "Have a pleasant flight." It was incredible! God's favour had been with us all the way there and back. God is amazing!

Saved By Grace

"For it is with your heart that you believe and are justified, and it is with your mouth that you profess your faith and are saved." Romans 10:10 (NIV)

The desire of every Christian parent is to know that their child has invited Jesus into their heart to be their Saviour. The Bible says in Proverbs 22:6 (NKJV) that we should:

"Train up a child in the way he should go, and when he is old, he will not depart from it."

We knew that we were not able to make any of our children invite Jesus into their hearts and lives. We could only teach them about Him, pray for them and hope that by our own example we could demonstrate how important Jesus is to us in our own lives.

Thankfully, before the age of six, each one of our precious children had made a decision to follow Jesus. They asked us on separate occasions, and each moment was extremely special. I cried with joy for each one of them. When Joshua was just four years old, he asked me how to become a Christian. We were in the car and had just arrived home. I told him that if we believe that Jesus died for us, that He rose from the dead and we have asked Him to forgive our sins, we can then ask Jesus to come into our lives and we will be saved. After my explanation, I started to get out of the car. He stopped me and told me that he wanted to pray that prayer right there and then, so he did. Luke 15:7 (NKJV) says:

> *"I say to you that likewise there will be more joy in heaven over one sinner who repents than over 99 just persons who need no repentance."*

I told him, as I had done with the others, that there was a huge party happening in Heaven because of the decision he had just made.

Camp Romain

> *"One way to get the most out of life is to look upon it as an adventure."*
> *William Feather*

Camp Romain

As a family we would often go to Camp Romain, which is an 8 km loop trail used for hiking, walking, running and nature trips in Le Rouret where we used to live.

Our children's primary school would often take their classes out on walks there, and once a year, the pupils would plant fruit trees, almond and olive trees or lavender bushes. Our children were very proud to show us which ones they had specifically planted. We would walk there regularly at the weekends. One Saturday, it was very windy, and the trees made such a noise that we had to talk louder to be able to hear one another. We had walked a long way, almost to the top of the hill, but then we thought we heard something. Was it a lamb bleating? It couldn't be; there weren't any sheep nearby, but what was that eerie crying noise? Perhaps it was a bird of prey of some sort? I left everyone on the path and clambered up through the rough prickly bushes and rocks to see where the noise was coming from, and then I saw a little boy. He was probably about four years old and must have been crying for a long time, as his face was covered in tears and dust, and he clearly looked distressed and exhausted.

I picked him up in my arms, but nervously wondered whether that was the best thing to do knowing that people could possibly accuse us of abducting him. He put his arms around my neck and hugged me close. Poor little thing must have been so grateful to have been rescued by us! We immediately phoned the police to tell them that we had found him. We started to make our way downhill and my top was wet from his runny nose, tears and his sweaty body. About 20 minutes later, we saw a family at a distance walking casually towards us. They didn't seem in any hurry, so I didn't think it could possibly be their son.

I stopped to put the little boy down to give my arms a break from holding him. At that point, there were two pathways to take back to the carpark. Our four children decided to take the more adventurous narrow path back. I picked the little boy up and continued to walk towards the family. The lady looked really surprised when she saw me holding her son. She had thought that her son was with her friends, and he had somehow got separated from them. They were not pleased when we told them that we had contacted the police, but we weren't going to take any risks.

On their way back, Samuel and Deborah had climbed up to look at something, and Rebecca and Joshua hadn't noticed that they were not walking behind them anymore, and had carried on together until they arrived at the carpark. When they arrived at the car, they found that they were on their own. They both were very distressed and burst into tears and started to walk back up the path to see if they could find us. Thankfully at the bottom of the hill, we came across all our children, some more distressed than others! It was so strange that we had helped someone who had lost their son and landed up losing our own children!

On another occasion, an October afternoon, our children had finished school for the day and asked me if we could walk up to Camp Romain to go and see the trees that they had planted. I agreed. It was about a half-hour walk to the top, maybe more. We spent time looking at the different trees and the shrubs that had been planted by them and their friends. I then looked at the time and realised it was about 5:00 p.m. It was time to make our way back. The path that we took was behind the hill and the sun was rapidly going down. It seemed to get dark very quickly and then we started hearing gunshots. The hunters were already out, looking for pheasants and boar. It was very disconcerting.

We started to walk a lot quicker, but the shooting seemed to get louder and more frequent. I was then aware that we were in a very dangerous spot and so I decided to tell the children that we needed to sing, and loudly so that the hunters could hear us. We sang songs together from the Doughnut man, "Jumping up and down, jumping up and down, jumping up and down, shout Hosanna, HOSANNA!" I was very nervous but tried not to show it. I was so relieved when we arrived back at the car and told them that we would never go back again to the Camp Romain so late in the afternoon.

Basketball

> *"You Can't Win Unless You Learn How To Lose."*
> *Kareem Abdul-Jabbar*

> *"Circumstances may appear to wreck our lives and God's plans, but God is not helpless among the ruins. God's love is still working. He comes in and takes the calamity and uses it victoriously, working out His wonderful plan of love."*
> *Eric Liddell*

Samuel loved playing basketball and he was in a very good team that played all over Nice. Unfortunately, sometimes the matches were on a Sunday, and they clashed with our church service. One day Samuel was told that his basketball team would be playing in an all-day Sunday tournament, and he asked us if he could play. We didn't want to disappoint him, but knew it was important to teach him that if we put God first in our lives, He would bless us. We agreed that he could join the team in the afternoon, but only if his trainer was happy with that. Thankfully she agreed. The difficult thing for Samuel, and for us, was that another boy in his team who also went to our church had been allowed by his parents to play in the whole tournament. I told Samuel that the boy's parents were entitled to make their own decisions before God, and that we had to make ours. I reminded him though, that I knew God would reward him in some way for putting Him first.

That Sunday we had a guest preacher in church. He decided to talk on giving, and to illustrate his topic he said, "The first person who answers this geography question correctly will get what is in my pocket." Samuel loved geography and was the first to put up his hand, answering the question correctly. He was given some money and was so happy.

I told him that if he hadn't come to church that morning, he would have missed out on getting the money. God had blessed him for putting Him first. As soon as the service was over, we hurried to Villeneuve Loubet where the tournament was held so that Samuel could join his team. On arrival we looked at the scoreboard. His team had lost every match until he arrived. As soon as he started playing, his team started to win and won the rest of the matches, apart from one! It was as if God said to Samuel, "You see, now that you have put Me first, I will bless your team." It reminded me of the story of Eric Liddell (from the 1981 film "Chariots of Fire") where he refused to run in a heat held on Sunday and was forced to withdraw from the 100-metre race, his best event. His friend reminded him of a Bible verse: *"But I will honour those who honour me."* 1 Samuel 2:30 (DBY). Later Eric Liddell went on to win gold in the 400-metre race in Paris in 1924.

Samuel in the centre with the blue jersey, number 4

September 2009 - Baptisms

> *"Parents can only give good advice or put them on the right paths, but the final forming of a person's character lies in their own hands."*
> *Anne Frank*

Our church announced that they would be organising their next baptism service (full immersion). Churches that perform christenings do so because of a decision of one's parents. However, water baptisms are a declaration of one's own personal faith and decision to follow Jesus. It was then that Samuel, our eldest child, asked us if he could get baptised. What a wonderful moment it was for us to know that our son wanted to make that important decision publicly - a statement to everyone that he had chosen to follow Jesus for the rest of his life. Paul was able to go into the water with Samuel and our pastor and they baptised him together.

09/26/2009 10:27

We stayed for quite a while after the baptisms as the children often liked to have fun swimming and playing games together. Joshua didn't want to swim, so he went to the bottom of the garden to play with some friends. Suddenly, we heard some terrible screaming and saw Joshua trying to make his way up the stairs in excruciating pain. He had fallen into a pile of dried palm branches that were waiting to be burnt, and two huge thick thorns had completely penetrated the area just below his bottom. He was forced to make the extremely painful journey up some 30 stairs to call for help. Thankfully, a friend of ours who is a professional firefighter was there and asked if anybody had any pliers in their car. It was impossible to get hold of the end of the thorns with one's fingers, or normal tweezers, as the thorns were so thick and completely embedded. He bent Joshua over his knee and with two sharp pulls, managed to dislodge the thorns and drew them out completely intact. One thorn was ten centimetres long, and the other, five centimetres! We could not believe our eyes when we saw what came out of him, and to think he had climbed those stairs! We had to take him to A & E at the hospital and they immediately disinfected the area and gave him a tetanus injection. We kept the thorns for a while, just so that he could tell his amazing story to his friends. We were so grateful he had no lasting injuries.

CHAPTER 22

An Unusual Skiing Holiday

*"What we fear doing most is usually
what we most need to do."*
Tim Ferriss

AT 52 YEARS OF AGE, with a wife and four children, Philippe Martinez was uncertain whether he should accept an invitation to guide a French expedition to the summit of Mount Everest. He had been a mountain guide since 1981 but had later become a Christian and subsequently a pastor and was no longer as reckless as he had been in his youth. After spending a year in rigorous training, Philippe and his team set off in April 2006 to scale the mountain. As they neared the summit, the report stated: "The weather conditions were favourable, and Philippe knew that God was leading the way. Indeed, he was so strong, both physically and spiritually, that he arrived at the summit 20 minutes ahead of the others. Taking off the oxygen mask, he began singing a hymn of praise. After being joined by the rest of his team, he made a symbolic gesture that, for him, was the sole purpose of the expedition. He buried his small Bible in the snow. In this way he wanted to show that God's Word was being proclaimed to the furthest reaches of the world. He also added a personal touch in the form of photos of his wife and children and a message, "Thank you, Lord, that You have protected me so far. I place into Your care those whom I love and I ask that my children will serve You one day." (5)

We had heard about Philippe through a friend. We booked a holiday one summer at a campsite in Die in the Drôme region near where he lived and arranged to meet up with him to hear his story. He became a friend of ours and invited Paul to preach at his church a couple of times. He is a skiing instructor, and his church is based close to a ski station called "Col du Rousset", which has stunning views over the Drôme valley. He invited us to go skiing with him in the February holidays and offered to give skiing lessons to our children. Finally, the winter holidays came, and we drove for four hours (taking the scenic route) to Die; the winding roads were sometimes slippery because of black ice and snow.

When we arrived at his church's guest apartment, we brought our suitcases inside and changed into our ski suits. Keen to start skiing, we then journeyed up the mountain, noticing that the higher we drove, the more cloud-cover there was. When we reached the ski lifts, we could no longer see any blue sky. It was extremely cold, and the wind had picked up too. Philippe told us to always stay close to him as the weather was deteriorating, and visibility wasn't great. We were honoured to have such a brilliant skiing instructor - perhaps one of the best in the world, knowing that he had climbed the Everest summit. As we had specifically gone to learn to ski, and were there only for a few days, we felt obliged to go skiing that day. We decided to do a "red" slope, which meant that we needed to take two sets of pommel lifts to get to the top. The metal poles we were holding were frozen, and I could see frost setting on the metal. When I moved my hands to get a better grip, I was aware of the material from my gloves sticking to the pole because it was so cold. Once there, we couldn't see further than two metres ahead of us. It was frightening, as we didn't know the ski slopes at all. Philippe explained that at the first slope we needed to go down rapidly, as it would immediately ascend. It was essential that we gained enough speed to get us to the top of the next slope. If we didn't descend fast enough, we would have to walk up with our skis.

As it was so cold and we couldn't see where we were going, we had to completely trust Philippe's word and follow him as closely as possible, not losing momentum. I was especially worried for our youngest children who were very inexperienced skiers, and I prayed none of us would fall on our way down. Amazingly, we all made it down and up again and quickly headed to the restaurant to warm ourselves up with hot chocolates and plates of hot chips to share. I wasn't very keen to venture out again, but remembering that we had paid quite a lot for the ski passes, I forced myself to go out again.

The next challenge was to take the chair lift to another ski slope. Rebecca and Joshua were no longer interested in skiing, so we left them inside the restaurant next to the warm fire. The wind was howling around my ears, and I had never experienced such a biting cold in my life. It was -19C, but the felt temperature was -39C!!! My fingers were burning and it was excruciatingly painful, and no matter how much I sat on them, rubbed them or blew into them to try to warm them up and get the circulation going, it didn't make any difference. Philippe was sitting next to me on the chair lift, and I showed him that my fingers were turning blue. He took out a pair of silk gloves he had inside his suit, which he said he used when he climbed Mount Everest. They were supposed to bring immediate relief to my fingers as they had been kept warm in his inside chest pocket. They didn't make any difference and by the look on Philippe's face, I knew I had to make a quick descent to save my fingers. He told me that my fingers had started their first stage of dying!

Deborah was keen to get back to the restaurant too, so we decided to go back together while Philippe, Paul and Samuel made a final run up the slopes. Philippe had explained to Deborah and me how to get back to the restaurant, but people who know me, know that I am not very good at directions! We had to go back on our skis cross-country, and after a while, it became too difficult to move forward anymore. We were obliged to take the skis off and walk, carrying them on our shoulders. It was very challenging as the snow had become hard and icy; we were exhausted, cold and starting to panic as we couldn't see clearly where we were going. Deborah started to cry and collapsed on the floor saying she couldn't go on any further as the skis were too heavy to carry. I had to be severe with her, as we both needed to keep up our strength to get back to the warmth. Finally, we could just make out a building ahead of us. I didn't recognise it at first, as we had come in from another way and had arrived from behind it.

Thankfully when we turned the corner, we realised it was the restaurant. We made our way to the front entrance and saw a man who had fallen over because of the icy snow, and he couldn't pull himself up. His wife started to call me for help, "Monsieur, monsieur." "Monsieur?!" I then realised that she thought I was a man as I was wearing a very thick male ski jacket and was much taller than her husband. I had to reach down to pull him up by his hand and nearly fell, as it was so slippery. I was glad I managed to keep my balance and we gingerly made our way into the restaurant. I couldn't wait to take my gloves off and to try to slowly get some warmth back into my greying fingers. The pain was incredible! We ordered a plate of hot chips and some hot chocolate and sat to thaw out. A few minutes later, the door to the restaurant opened and a gentleman with a big French moustache came inside. His nose had obviously been running from the cold and had frozen leaving a huge icicle hanging down off his moustache. It was hilarious! Moments later, another lady came in complaining that she could hardly see, and she felt as if her eyes had frozen. It seemed like a very long time before the others came back and I was so relieved to finally see them. I found out that Samuel had decided he wanted to go up the slope one final time, and without telling Philippe or Paul, was already on his way up without them. You can imagine that they were not too pleased with him, but thankfully he wasn't too far ahead, and they were able to accompany him safely back down again. We all sat together at the table with our hot drinks and talked about our experiences. Philippe told us that the temperatures we had experienced were similar to those on the Everest and he said, "Today, you did not climb Mount Everest, but this was your Everest."

As the following day was Sunday, Philippe was preaching, and he asked Paul and I to say something to the congregation before his sermon. We talked about our experience skiing the previous day and told them how much we had been obliged to put our complete trust in their pastor. We explained that we could relate the experiences of that day to our life and trusting God. We do not know what life will bring or what challenges we will face, but God knows what is best for us and He clearly knows the path we should take in life. We can trust Him fully, knowing that He will guide us and take us to a safe place. *"Even when the way goes through Death Valley, I'm not afraid when you walk at my side. Your trusty shepherd's crook makes me feel secure." Psalm 23:4 (MSG).*

CHAPTER 23

Coincidence Or God-incidence?

Then the LORD took Abram outside and said to him, "Look up into the sky and count the stars if you can. That's how many descendants you will have."
Genesis 15:5 (NLT)

29 OCTOBER 2010: This day was a double blessing for our family. Deborah had decided two months previously that she wanted to be baptised, and Grandad and Granny (who were now living in the UK), had planned to visit us for that special occasion. Interestingly, their church home group had been discussing baptisms and asked who had been baptised.

My dad hadn't been baptised but had started thinking about it. Deborah phoned him and asked if he would like to be baptised on the same day as her, and without hesitation, he agreed. It was an incredible celebration. Both Deborah and her Granddad were baptised that day by our pastor and Paul.

Halloween, October 2010

*"We must build dikes of courage to
hold back the flood of fear."
Martin Luther King, Jr.*

On Sunday the 31st of October 2010, on our way home from our church service, our car broke down. It was pouring sheets of rain and we sat in the car for a long time waiting for a tow truck to rescue us. A friend's son was with us in the car; he was going to sleepover at our home. I felt so sorry for him as it was no fun sitting with us. We were hungry and cold, and I desperately needed to go to the toilet. The tow truck took so long to arrive that I had to knock on the door of a nearby house and ask them to allow me to use the bathroom. It was so embarrassing. Eventually the tow truck came, the man jumped out his truck and without telling us to get out of our car, hoisted us up - all seven of us still sitting in the car! The car rocked precariously from side to side as it was manoeuvred onto the truck. He didn't get out to see if we were ok, but immediately slammed his door shut, started the engine and began driving. We swayed and jolted around, and it was scary looking out of the window and seeing how high above the road we were! He drove for ten minutes and then stopped in Valbonne village. He climbed out of his truck and helped us all to get out. He told us that we had to take all our belongings with us and that we were to make our way to the bus stop shelter, as he wasn't allowed to take us any further. I had my Bible in one hand and violin in the other. The rain was pouring down heavily, and water was swirling around our feet as we rushed to the bus stop. The ground was saturated, and it was impossible to find a dry patch to put my violin down. We phoned for a taxi, but as the weather was so bad, the taxi took one and a half hours to rescue us, all the while holding onto my violin!

We eventually arrived home, cold, wet and hungry. We then discovered that we had run out of gas to turn the radiators on, so I quickly made a fire, and we all sat in front of it trying to warm up and dry out. After eating a light snack, we went to bed early as we were all so tired. Suddenly, around 3 a.m., Paul woke me up with a loud shout. "What's that noise?" "Water's coming through the light above our head!" "No, it's not," I said, "It's just the noise from the radiator." Then suddenly I understood what he had said and woke up with a jolt. Water was indeed coming out of the light fitting above our head! I tried to run up the stairs to find out where the water was coming from, and to my horror, slipped halfway up as water was trickling down them. When I went into the lounge, water was swirling around my feet. For some reason I said out loud, "The Lord gives, and the Lord takes away." Don't ask me why I said that it just came out! I shouted out to the kids, who were sleeping upstairs, to come and help. They were fast asleep, but soon woke up. With the lounge lights on, we opened the door leading out to our second veranda on the opposite side of the lounge and started to sweep the water out. It was coming in from the front door and rushing down the stairs into our lounge. I couldn't believe my eyes when I saw how much water was coming into the house. Ridiculously, and without thinking, I opened the front door to see what was going on and where the water was coming from; I obviously hadn't woken up properly! Yes, you guessed it - a lot more water came in a whole lot quicker! 60 cm of rain had accumulated on the front terrace and was rapidly pouring in through the front door.

With great difficulty I pushed the door closed again to stop the force of water rushing in. I cautiously made my way down the stairs trying not to slip again but going as fast as I possibly could. My aim was to grab as many towels as I could find and to stuff them behind the front door, easing the flow of water and giving us time to sweep the water out the other side of the house, keeping the water level from rising above the electricity sockets on the walls. Finally, after several hours of sweeping the water out the other door, the rain stopped and the drains outside started coping with the sheer amount of rain, and the water stopped coming in.

We went down the stairs to check the damage and turned the light on without thinking; the lightbulb had been sitting in a pool of water for several hours but was still working! Water had managed to seep through the cracks in the lounge floor to the two bedrooms below, and our clothes and linen in the cupboards were sopping wet. Incredibly though, water had leaked through several different areas in the ceiling but there wasn't one drop on our mattress! We were so grateful that it was still dry. Amazingly, while we worked to stop the house from flooding, the electricity and lights still functioned which helped us to see what we were doing. It was only afterwards that we realised we had been working in an extremely dangerous situation. All of us had been standing in water barefoot in the lounge, and we could have been electrocuted. We were not aware that the trip switch couldn't work in our house, as the electrical switchboard had been installed without an earth wire!

Friends from church kindly offered to wash and dry all the towels we had used to stop the water coming in, as well as all the clothes and linen that were drenched in our cupboards. A lady from the insurance came in a few days later to inspect the damage. We were given the option of having a professional painter come to do the work for us, or for the insurance to pay us a lump sum of money so that we could do the painting ourselves. We chose the latter.

We realised that the flood had been a huge blessing in disguise, as financially we were really struggling to pay the bills. We were able to buy paint and brushes, gloves and painting overalls for a very reasonable price. We hired dehumidifiers and bought gas to heat the house. When the house was finally dry, we repainted it and had quite a lot of money left over to pay the bills during that difficult season.

A Slippery Slope

On another cold and rainy day, I decided to take the children out to the Monoprix shopping centre in Grasse. I drove into the spiral parking garage and continued down to the basement, as there were no parking spaces available on the ground level. We made our way to the shops and had fun looking at the wide range of food, home and fashion products. Eventually we decided it was time to go back to the car. As I began to drive up the slope to get to the ground level, the car slid back down again as it was icy and extremely slippery. I reversed to try again so that I could get a bit more speed to drive up the slope. Just at that moment, another car arrived and tried to drive up.

We watched in horror as the same thing happened to them, but this time they narrowly missed sliding into a cement wall. I tried a second time and our car slid back down again; it was very alarming. In hindsight, I should have gone to speak to a staff member in the shop. The thought didn't even cross my mind, as I was just determined to get out of there. I then decided to walk with my children up to the ground floor level and told them to hold hands and stand behind a parked car, so that they would be safe. I quickly ran back down to the car and reversed it as far as possible. Taking a deep breath, I then put my foot flat on the accelerator and sped up the slope as quickly as I could with the wheels spinning and smoking. Thankfully this time I made it! I stopped just near where I had left the children and piled them all back into the car as hastily as possible. I was worried that someone might speed up the ramp like I did and crash into us. After that alarming experience, I vowed I would never go to that car park again. I was shaking and emotionally drained when we arrived home but was extremely thankful that we were safe and that our car was dent free.

CHAPTER 24

Walking Like
A Crab

"The Sovereign LORD is my strength!
He makes me as surefooted as a deer,
able to tread upon the heights."
Habakkuk 3:19 (NLT)

FOR JUST OVER SIX YEARS, I had been suffering
from sciatica and it seemed to start just after the birth
of our fourth child. The pain became very severe to the
point where I needed quite a lot of anti-inflammatory
medication; X-rays were taken to see why. The
specialist found out that part of my cartilage had been
worn away, and that explained why I was really
struggling to walk. My hip would get stuck when

walking, and to avoid severe pain, I would have to walk sideways and drag my leg with me. An appointment had been made with the hip surgeon to discuss having a hip replacement operation done, and I needed to wait a couple of months to see him. After doing a lot of research, I found out that although a hip replacement is a fairly simple procedure, I would have to have another hip replacement done ten years later if I was to go ahead with the surgery. I decided to ask people in my women's Bible study group to pray for me and to ask God to heal me.

Shortly after that, Paul and I went to a conference where we sat next to someone who talked to me about the benefits of drinking alkaline water. As our diet can be very acidic, he mentioned that this would help me. I started to notice a big difference after buying the ioniser. The pain was much less, and I was able to eventually stop taking all medication, which by then was nine different types to help ease the pain. The day finally arrived for me to meet the surgeon. He showed me a model hip and explained how the procedure was to be done and what the result would be. He then said to me, "The next time I see you, will be for the hip operation." My reply was, "Thank you very much Doctor, but I hope that I will never need to see you again." He looked very surprised. I had already noticed a change in my hip, and I knew that with prayer and a change of diet, my hip was getting better. A few months later, we had 20cm of snow fall on the mountains. Our children asked us if we could go and do some sledging in the snow. I was a bit worried about how my hip would hold out, but we walked for hours in the snow, and in some parts, the snow was very deep, and I had to lift my one leg out of the snow completely, take a big step forward and then pull the other leg out. I managed really well without any pain and when we came home, I realised that even after several hours of exercise, I had no feeling at all of strain or pain in my legs or hips. (Ten years later, my hip is still fine. I have had the odd twinge of pain, but I am medication-free and have not had a hip operation). Once again, God worked another miracle in me!

Seeing The Funny Side Of Things

"A sense of humour... is needed armour. Joy in one's heart and some laughter on one's lips is a sign that the person down deep has a pretty good grasp of life." Hugh Sidey

During the week on the way to school we would often listen to a local radio station called "Riviera Radio". One day I heard an announcement about a joke competition. People could enter the competition by phoning in and telling their favourite joke. It was recorded, and if the presenters liked it, it would be played sometime during the week. If, however, they thought your joke was the best, it would be played on the Friday morning for a second time, and you could win one of their amazing prizes. Each Monday morning, they would announce what the prize would be for the week. One week the prize was a €150 gift voucher to spend at a garden centre and shop. I thought this would be a brilliant prize to enter for, as if I won, I could use the voucher to buy some flour for our bread machine, along with other needed items from the shop.

On the Friday morning I eagerly listened in and heard my recorded joke. I couldn't believe that I had won, and it was so easy to do. I won many prizes that year. One prize was a free lunch for eight people at a newly opened English restaurant. My parents were visiting at the time, so we were able to take them and our whole family out for lunch. Another prize I won was a dinner for two at a golf club called "Chateau de la Begude" in Opio with a five-star restaurant not far from where we lived.

Chateau de la Begude

Another prize was for six people to eat at a restaurant located in Saint-Jean-Cap-Ferrat, a seaside village on a peninsula jutting into the Mediterranean

Sea between Nice and Monaco. We took all our children out for this treat. Paul also decided to see if he could win a prize. We found a good joke for him to tell, and each Monday we would listen to see if it was a prize that he would want to win. He practised his joke on me repeatedly until it was perfect. That Monday, they announced that the prize would be an iPad. Paul thought it would be a very useful prize, so he called in with his joke.

On the Friday morning we hurriedly turned on the radio, eager to see if Paul's joke was going to be played. Just before announcing the winner, the presenter said that the prize had been changed and would be a three-month subscription to a local fitness club. Paul won and we laughed so much! No excuses then - he would have to go and do some exercise! It turned out to be an incredible prize, as it was extended to a 12-month free subscription.

It was amazing for us that even though we were struggling so much financially, God was blessing us with these prizes, enabling us to take our family out to dinner and have wonderful trips as a couple.

The best prize that we won was bed and breakfast for two at "Chateau de Berne", situated in the Var region with a beautiful vineyard, wine tasting, a lovely swimming pool and beautiful scenery. We saw ostriches there, which reminded me of Zimbabwe, and we were able to play tennis as well. Part of the prize was being able to choose our own room. It was a fabulous treat!

Chateau de la Begude

A Golden Miracle

The fantastic thing about living in the South of France was that we could drive to the beaches on our free afternoons, or at weekends, as it was only a 20-minute drive away. The beaches were lovely, and the children spent many hours playing in the sun. One outing we will never forget was when Paul decided to take the children by himself to the beach as I had to work in our "gîte". He took them to a pebbly beach near Villeneuve Loubet called "Baie des Anges" (Bay of Angels).

The kids loved taking their goggles with them to look for fish and small crabs that popped out of their shells. After a couple of hours playing, Deborah and Rebecca were suddenly approached by an anxious looking man who announced that he had lost his wedding ring in the sea! He told them roughly where it had fallen off and asked them to look for it with their goggles. Well as you well know, looking for anything in the sea is challenging. Once, my jelly shoe slipped off my foot and I tried to grab it and it was extremely difficult to see where it had gone. The girls began to look under water, but the current was so strong that they soon found themselves in a different spot to where they had started. The pebbles were swirling around their feet and were being tossed frantically backwards and forwards by the waves.

Deborah was the only one in the family that needed prescription glasses. She didn't have her glasses on and was straining to see through her goggles. She stood up again to take a breath, and then prayed and asked God to help her to find the wedding ring. She felt God tell her to start digging, and suddenly, she saw something gold. She picked it up... it was a gold ring! She ran to the man and asked him if it was his ring.

He couldn't believe it! The relief must have been incredible. He explained that he had bought his wedding ring in Monaco, and knowing that, I am sure that it didn't only have sentimental value! He ran to tell his family and came back with 20 euros to give to Deborah, telling her that she would never be able to understand just how relieved he was to have his ring back. She was so happy and ran to put her money away in her bag. When she turned around, she was surprised to see him running back to her again with a further 10 euros. He wanted to express his gratitude, and this was the only way possible. 30 euros for an answer to prayer;

a golden miracle done with no glasses, but a lot of help from God!

Is It Raining Again?

After the first experience of flooding in our home, every time it rained heavily after that, I found it extremely difficult to relax. We had called the plumber in to clear out the drain next to our terrace and front door as they didn't drain well when our house had flooded. He unblocked the drain and discovered several tennis balls and ping-pong balls that had clogged up the pipes. The previous owners had obviously used the terrace to play ping-pong and had never recuperated the balls when they had fallen into the drain. We also discovered another pipe that had been covered up by soil (after several years of erosion) and could no longer drain away the water from the terrace near our swimming pool. We cleaned out all the gutters and hoped that we had done enough to stop the house flooding again.

A couple of months later at about 3 a.m., Paul woke me up with a shout. "What's that noise?" "What noise?!!" "I don't hear anything," … and then I did! Water was gushing from somewhere, but where? It wasn't in our bedroom - we could just hear it. "The POOL!!!" "The POOL!!" I put my shoes on, grabbed my dressing gown, and ran outside into the dark and down to the swimming pool pump room. The pump room backed onto Joshua's bedroom which was next to ours, and as our rooms were in the basement, we could hear the rushing sound of water clearly. I hurried into the room to find out what was going on. Water was gushing all over the place, and then I saw the problem... The pipe which takes the water from the bottom of the pool and feeds it back into the pump had snapped, and the pool was emptying all over the pump and the electrical control panel! Imagining the worst, I knew that I could get electrocuted standing there anyway, so I reached up and turned the power off and was struck by a sudden electric shock up my arm! Thankfully I lived to tell the tale - God obviously hadn't finished with me yet! We somehow managed to change some valves to stop the water flowing and called the swimming pool technician in later that day to fix the broken pipe.

"Pride deafens us to the advice or warnings of those around us."
John C. Maxwell

It was a Wednesday and in France, schools close in the afternoons. The children were home and playing on the terrace and Paul was out at work. The sky grew darker by the minute and then rain began to fall heavily. The drops were so huge that they looked like hail. Then the drops turned into a sheet of rain so thick, that you could not see through it. I had never seen anything like it, and in Africa where I come from, rain used to fall very heavily. Le Rouret, our village, was in the centre of the storm. Lightning flashed and immediately we heard the thunder. Within ten minutes the rain was struggling to flow through the drains in the garden and on our terrace, and 20 minutes later, it was as though a mini tsunami had arrived on our doorstep. Water from the neighbour's garden above us came over the "restanque" (drywall terrace), perhaps 20 cm in height by that stage, and continued to accumulate. As we were all on the terrace, we grabbed buckets and brooms and did whatever we could to keep the water away from the front door. We were fighting a losing battle. It was just impossible to work against the huge quantity of water coming down the hill.

While we were working on the terrace, and once again barefoot, I noticed an extension lead that was lying 20cm underwater right where I was standing. I realised that we were all at risk of being electrocuted and knew I had to get it out of the water immediately. I bent down and picked it up, and as I was placing it on top of the fridge, immediately felt that familiar feeling from the previous flooding - a huge electric shock right up my right arm. Incredibly I survived that too! I didn't think anything more of it, but just continued to sweep the water away in vain, as frantically as possible. In desperation, I phoned the firemen to ask them to come and help suck up the water, which by that time was now inside the house. They told us that two boys had been washed off their feet by a strong current of water coming from a large open water drain. They had been swept into the swollen waters of a nearby river, and one of the brothers had died. Forty firemen had been working to rescue them and because of that, they were unable to come and help us. I realised then how grateful I was that we were all still alive and that although our house had been flooded once again, we hadn't lost a life in our household. One of the boys had been in Deborah's class at school, and the fact that she knew him made it even worse. This incident was the talk of the town and people were asking questions like, "What kind of a God would allow this to happen?" One person told us though, that an elderly lady had seen them near the river. She had noticed the approaching storm, and had told them to go inside, but they hadn't heeded her warning. I believe God had sent her to warn them in advance, but they unfortunately didn't want to listen.

17 September 2011 - Baptisms Again

Once again, our church announced another baptism service and asked if there was anyone who wanted to get baptised. Rebecca asked if she could speak to us on her own in Paul's office. She said that she wanted to get baptised and didn't want anyone in the house to overhear what she was saying. She explained that she had heard the message in church and really wanted to get baptised. We were very happy with her decision but kept it quiet from the others. We were glad we did, as a few days later Joshua did a similar thing. He came to us when no one was around and said he had been thinking about getting baptised as he had heard the announcement in church. He was seven and a half years old, and I wondered if he was too young. I asked him what it meant to get baptised, and he very easily explained it to us. We didn't give him an answer straight away, as we told him that we would pray about it. I went away and asked God if Joshua was too young and He reminded me of this verse:

> *But Jesus said, "Let the children come to me.*
> *Don't stop them! For the Kingdom of Heaven*
> *belongs to those who are like these children."*
> *Matthew 19:14 (NLT)*

I had the answer. We should never refuse a child who wants to draw closer to God. Once again, we had a double celebration and Rebecca, and Joshua were baptised. Our prayers had always been that each one of our children would one day make their own personal decision to follow Jesus. All four of our precious children had made that decision because they had experienced Jesus's love for them. Our hearts were bursting with joy, and we were so thankful. We had explained to them that as parents we were not perfect, and we would make mistakes in bringing them up, but God will never let them down. He will give them the wisdom that they need to live their lives well.

Joshua Keeps Us On Our Toes

There were a series of food and petrol shortages as strikes were becoming more common in France. Truck drivers blocked motorways, which in turn stopped food getting to the shops. Paul suggested that it would be a good idea to stock up and have a food supply at home just in case. We decided to go and buy a large quantity of powdered milk, tinned food, pasta and rice; a family of six needs a lot of food for one week. We all went to the shops as the children wanted to help us. Once the shopping was done, Paul put all the shopping bags next to the car so that he could work out the best way of putting them in.

Joshua was wanting to help as well, but the bags were too heavy for him to lift. As he was walking around the bags, his little foot caught in one of the handles that was lying on the floor, and he fell back on his head. I could 'hear' the fall. I rushed to help him and put my hand at the back of his head. Warm blood started to trickle out between my fingers, and I could feel his head pulsating, which was alarming and very unpleasant. I found a pack of clean tissues and pressed those gently, but firmly on his head to try to stop the bleeding. We prayed for him and eventually the bleeding stopped, and we were all able to drive home.

When we arrived, we cleaned his head with disinfectant and warm water but noticed the wound was quite big and unsightly. Realising it probably needed a better clean at the hospital, we took him there and discovered that he needed stitches. They had to inject a local anaesthetic into the back of his head which was painful, but that enabled the doctor to do the stitches. We were glad when that day was finally over!

CHAPTER 25

Itchy Feet

"It's time to say goodbye, but I think goodbyes are sad and I'd much rather say hello. Hello to a new adventure."
Ernie Harwell

2012: AFTER ALMOST SEVEN YEARS of living in the South of France and serving the church there, we started to feel unsettled. There had been a number of changes in our church, and the American pastor that had faithfully led it when we first arrived, had died. We began to wonder if it was time for us to leave France.

Back in 2010, Paul had thought a lot about Canada and us moving there as a family to live. I had never been there before but have cousins living in Toronto and they kindly invited us to stay with them for two weeks. We were able to visit Niagara Falls and do some camping, but the main reason for going there of course was to see if we should immigrate. With this thought always in my mind, I could not really enjoy our holiday there. Instead of feeling excited about the prospects of making Toronto our home, I was uneasy about it and didn't like the idea of being far away from our family in Europe. We visited a church and did some job and house-hunting there, but on our return to France, made the decision not to move there. It was an enormous relief for me.

The next option we considered was moving to Geneva in Switzerland. We visited a church there and wondered if moving there would offer us a better future. The door didn't open there either and we therefore continued asking God to show us where He wanted us to live. On the 22nd of April 2012, the presidential elections were held in France. After all the votes had been cast, we sat in front of the television with our eyes glued to the screen. First Nicolas Sarkozy's face appeared on the screen and then Francois Hollande's and then Sarkozy's. This pattern continued for several minutes until finally the screen froze on Francois Hollande. This confirmed that he was the newly elected president. It made us feel even more unsure of our future in France.

Just a few days later, Paul was praying, and he remembered the name of an English pastor who had visited our local church six years previously. Paul explained to me what had happened during his prayer time and wondered whether perhaps God was giving us an opportunity to return to England. England? When I first heard that, I thought he was crazy! I asked him why God would possibly call us back to England and reminded him of our initial calling to go to France. Why would God call us to France, allow us to go through all the struggles, learn the language, adapt to the culture - to call us back again to the UK? It just didn't make sense.

The pastor from England had come to lead a men's weekend retreat and Paul had translated for him. When the weekend was over, we didn't think about him again. Paul found out from a Google search that this pastor was based in a church in Surrey, just outside London. We decided to speak to our own pastor to discuss our plans to visit the UK, and to ask him for some advice. The day after Paul felt we should visit the UK, he phoned the pastor in Surrey and explained what had happened while he was praying and asked if we could possibly visit his church the following week. 'By coincidence', that weekend was a long weekend, so Paul didn't have to take time off work. I was dreading telling my family about the possibility of us moving back to the UK. Just what would they think? I could almost hear it… "Weren't you called as missionaries to France?" Are you sure you have heard from God?" "How can you take the children away from their friends and their country?"

I prayed to God, asking Him to show me if we were really meant to leave our beloved France. Actually, I don't think I really wanted to hear God's answer, as I was convinced that Paul couldn't possibly have heard right this time. Looking back, however, I realised that each time we moved, our situation improved. This time though, I was so worried that we were wrong. I decided to give God a chance to speak to me and so we booked our flights to England and five days later we arrived there. At Gatwick airport, we went through passport control and made our way to find the car rental company. We called the lift; the door opened, and the sun came shining in. The sun was so warm on my face, and believe it or not, that weekend it was warmer in London than in the South of France! As soon as I saw the sun, I immediately 'heard in my spirit' an English expression, *"Make hay while the sun shines."* It had been over 16 years since we had lived in the UK, and I don't think I had thought about, or used any English expressions while living in France. I turned to Paul in the lift and said questioningly, "Make hay while the sun shines?" "What are you talking about?" he asked. Well, I had to explain that this time it was me 'hearing' things in my spirit. Paul hadn't heard of that expression before, and I had to explain to him its meaning: "Make the most of the opportunity while you have it." I then realised that this time God was speaking to me, showing me that the move to the UK was right for us.

The pastor in Surrey was so accommodating and organised for us to stay with a South African lady from his church. He also arranged for us to meet a Dutch couple who had four children; they gave us helpful information on schooling. We also met a businessman and his wife, a GP, who listened to our business ideas, giving us hope that they would be feasible. We also attended a church service which was just so much fun.

At the church service they were showing a movie; it was an event they called "Movie May." Drinks and popcorn were given out and four clips were shown from the movie. The pastor used the clips to illustrate themes from the Bible. It was the most refreshing church service we had ever been to. I looked around at the people in the church, thinking about the possibility of making that church our home; we had been given a wonderful welcome. The only concern I had was for our daughter Deborah, as I didn't see any girls her age. I knew that if God wanted us to move, He would look after the details that were important to us as a family.

On our return to France that Bank holiday Monday, we both felt that the trip had been beneficial and successful; it was as if God had rolled out the red carpet to us. We met up with our pastor again and told him that we had decided to return to the UK permanently. That same week, just a few days later, President Hollande met with the Prime Minister of the UK at that time, Mr Cameron, in Downing Street. Mr Cameron said to him, "I'm rolling out the red carpet to any French businessmen who want to come to the UK." It made us laugh. I know we are not French, but we had some business ideas and the fact that we were coming from France made us feel that even the Government in the UK was welcoming us. To top it all, Paul was reading his Bible that same week and he came across a passage from The Message translation, and this is what he read:

"Make hay while the sun shines—that's smart; go fishing during harvest—that's stupid." Proverbs 10:5 (MSG).

It was more than just a coincidence for us, and I was amazed that the expression was in the Bible. When we were completely sure about our decision, we dropped the bombshell on our families. I was right; they asked all the questions I had been asking myself, but I knew that they were only asking them because they loved us and wanted the best. I have learned though, that what matters most is to follow God's leading and not to worry about what others think. I trusted Him, that in time, He would show them that we had heard correctly.

We decided to repaint our house and managed to finish redecorating it in two weeks. After that we went to an estate agent and put our house on the market. Altogether we had 77 visits of potential buyers to the house. Finally, a young couple came and fell in love with it; we arranged for the signing at the solicitor's office. On arrival, we waited excitedly to sign the papers for the sale of our house. Unfortunately, when we saw the solicitor, she explained to our horror that part of the land in our garden, which was within the fenced boundary, didn't belong to us as we had initially believed. It belonged to the neighbours that were just a bit further down the hill below us.

The surveyor had made a mistake when the houses were first built and had drawn the boundary line in the wrong place on the plans and we hadn't been informed of this when we bought it. Instead of drawing the boundary line where our fence was, he had drawn it in the middle of our garden! We therefore had to postpone the signing. We arranged to meet with our neighbours to discuss the land issue. They agreed to sell the land to us for €1, as the land boundaries had been drawn up 15 years previously. As the land was two metres above their own property, it was useless to them. We agreed with the future buyers to sort out the paperwork and rescheduled the date. Two weeks later we went back to the solicitor's office again. The legal documents still hadn't been sorted out, but the buyers agreed to sign, knowing that they could pull out of the sale before the end of the three-month period if they hadn't been processed accordingly. As they had signed to buy our home, we knew that it was finally possible to leave France, trusting that the issue with the land would be ironed out easily, and our house sale would go through.

The pastor's wife in England had suggested to us that we should rent a house in Esher (Surrey), which would enable us to be in the right catchment area for our children to go to the best government schools. The Dutch family that we had met, kindly went to visit a house that we were interested in renting. They took several photos of it, and without us physically seeing the house before leaving France, we signed the rental agreement, and it was approved. We planned to arrive in England mid-December, and the money from the sale of the house was expected to come through at the end of January, enabling us to settle into our new home in England. That would then give Paul the time he needed to look for work without any financial pressures.

"A time to weep, and a time to laugh; a time to mourn, and a time to dance." Ecclesiastes 3:4 (NIV)

It seemed like our plans were working out well. We had found buyers for the house, had a house to move into in England and had applied for places for our children in the local schools there. We just needed someone to buy our car. I had the incredible task of packing all our belongings into boxes, and of course selling things we didn't need any longer. I chose only one pot plant to take with us as a reminder of the house in Le Rouret.

One day, I had just sold one of my favourite oak shelving units that we had been given by a very kind lady, and out of the blue, all the memories from our time in France came flooding back. I wearily sat down, emotions high. I thought of the different churches we had been involved in, the children's ministry, the marriage ministry, the floods, the moves from one house to another, the financial pressures, the friends we had made, the reasons we had come to France, the lady who had given her life to Jesus… There were so many dreams and good intentions, so many wonderful happy memories, but so many things we aspired to do that were left unfulfilled, and then… A tear trickled down my face, then another, and soon I found myself sobbing uncontrollably. I sobbed and sobbed and sobbed, as if my heart would break. I cried for my beloved France, the place where our precious children were born. Were these doors finally closing forever? I cried for the disappointments, for the friends that we had made that we wouldn't see regularly anymore. I realised that I was in a time of mourning, but it was OK. As it says in Ecclesiastes, *"There is a time for everything,"* and God was there with me in the middle of it all. It was important that I went through it. It was important that I expressed my feelings and thoughts, enabling me to leave my past behind me and to move on to the bright future that God had prepared. All in all, it lasted about two weeks, and then one morning, I realised that my heart was no longer heavy. It was as if a huge black cloud from a storm had blown away. I was at peace. It was a new dawn, and rest had entered my heart that day and I started looking forward to our new life in the UK.

Selling Our Car To Pay For The Removal Costs

"Some of us think holding on makes us strong; but sometimes it is letting go." Hermann Hesse

Our Ford Galaxy had been with us for almost a year, and we thoroughly enjoyed driving it. When we had bought it, it was just a few months old. It had been delivered to our door all the way from Germany. Now it was time to sell it as we needed to pay for our home contents to be transported to London. Two months before leaving, we put up some adverts around the shops, and on various websites. We received only two calls - one from a lady who realised it wasn't what she was looking for, and another from a gentleman who sounded very interested, but didn't come to see it. We were getting very worried as the removal company told us that we had to pay them two weeks before the removal date. If we didn't pay on time, the booking would be cancelled, and we would have to reschedule our move to the UK. We knew it was imperative to move on that date, as if the move was postponed, we would lose the home we had put a deposit on in England. Just three days before we were due to pay the removal company, the gentleman called back. He apologised for not getting in touch with us again, but explained that there had been some illnesses in the family, and it had delayed his visit to see the car. He arranged to come the following day and brought the cash with him just in case he decided to buy it. Thankfully he loved it, and we were able to pay the removal company just in time. It had all been very stressful.

Three days flew by and then I heard a removal van reversing down our driveway. Our road was too narrow to allow a huge removal truck down it, so a smaller Luton van had been sent. In three trips, they managed to transport all our belongings to their depot, where they transferred everything into one huge removal truck ready to go.

CHAPTER 26

So Long, Farewell, Auf Wiedersehen, Adieu

> *"When it's time for you to venture out,
> don't let fear have you looking back on
> what you're leaving behind."*
> *Anonymous*

SUNDAY THE NINTH OF DECEMBER 2012 was our last Sunday in church. We had been part of that church for over six years, and it was hard to say goodbye to all our friends and the children that we had taught. We were called up to the front of the congregation so that the leaders could pray for our family and for our imminent move to the UK. It was very moving, no pun intended 😊. I don't think people really understood just how difficult it was for us to leave France, but we had made the decision, and had to leave the past behind us. Some lovely friends in the church had offered us their apartment to stay in for our last few days in the country. It was special being with such supportive friends during our final few days. We said our goodbyes, left the church for the last time and went back to the apartment to mull over the events of the day. While relaxing, Paul started to read some emails that had come in. He noticed we had received one from someone in the church. They began by saying that they had chosen not to attend our farewell service but had waited outside in the coffee area until the service was over. This person had decided not to come as they did not agree with us leaving France. They could not believe that we would "flee from the country that had welcomed us, given us freedom to worship and a good education for our children." They also judged us for the reasons why we were leaving, which they believed were political and because of economic instability. They were unaware that God had spoken to both Paul and I on separate occasions, and it was only because of His leading that we had made the decision to go.

It was a real blow to us, and we felt like someone had punched us in the stomach. They had no idea how much pain we were experiencing as we prepared to leave the country that had been ours for almost 17 years. We had chosen to obey God and to leave France even though it was difficult and we didn't know what lay ahead. This was yet another person we had to forgive immediately.

"Then Peter came to him and asked, "Lord, how often should I forgive someone who sins against me? Seven times?" No, not seven times," Jesus replied, "but seventy times seven!" Matthew 18:21-22 (NLT)

As we had sold our car, we had to hire an eight-seater Mercedes minibus to transport us to England. We needed the extra room so that we could take our cat and rabbit too. It was an exhausting trip that took two days. The vet had given us some medicine to help the cat relax while travelling. The tablet only seemed to kick in once we arrived at the hotel after a full-day's drive! He meowed and whined throughout the whole journey. It was stressful for us and very stressful for him too, but the rabbit didn't seem to mind. We took the cat into the hotel room in his dog crate which we had bought so that he would have room to move around. He absolutely hated being in the hotel and made some very strange and disturbing noises throughout the night. We finally woke up after an unrestful night's sleep, climbed back into the minibus and drove to Calais to get the Eurotunnel shuttle which would take us to Folkestone. Once on the train, it stopped and started and jerked in that same manner for the entire journey. We could hear a terrible noise of screeching brakes and it felt like something was trying to hold us back from getting to England. We were eventually told that the brakes had overheated and that the train had to move slowly so that the brakes didn't catch fire. A journey that should have taken 35 minutes took five hours! After finally arriving on English soil, we made our way to a hotel in Twickenham (South West London), where we spent one more night there. The following morning, we were finally able to get the keys to our new home in Esher, Surrey.

Our next adventure had begun in the UK. Had we heard correctly from God? Would we adapt easily to our new life and rapidly find employment? Would the children be given places in the schools we had applied to? How would we settle in our new church? Would the money come through from the sale of our house? Would our children like it and make friends? There were so many unanswered questions. It was a big leap of faith, but we had done it. Now we had to trust God to take care of the rest. *"Therefore put on the full armour of*

God, so that when the day of evil comes, you may be able to stand your ground, and after you have done everything, to stand."
Ephesians 6:13 (NIV)

Thanks for taking an interest in our own personal walk with God. I couldn't possibly write everything that happened in those 16.5 years, however, you now have some idea of what it was like for us to follow God's lead, serving Him as faithfully as possible, while enjoying and living life to the full.

As this book goes to print, our family had the privilege of visiting Hillsong church in Lyon recently. It is so encouraging to see what God is doing in that city. We went to visit our daughter Deborah who was offered a job there for six months to gain work experience as part of her degree. She had joined Hillsong church, auditioned to sing in their worship band, and was immediately rostered on to sing regularly during her stay there. Hillsong Lyon had opened its doors in 2014 and now has more than 300 members.

When we left Lyon to live in the South of France many years ago, I was sad to leave, and God gave me the following Bible verse to hold on to:

"Those who plant in tears will harvest with shouts of joy.
They weep as they go to plant their seed, but they sing
as they return with the harvest."
Psalm 126:5-6 (NLT)

Isn't it amazing that the person from our family who returned to Lyon was the one who sings! I love that! While our daughter was there, God gave me a verse for her:

"After consulting the people, the king appointed singers to walk ahead of the army, singing to the Lord and praising him for his holy splendour. This is what they sang: "Give thanks to the Lord; his faithful love endures forever!"
2 Chronicles 20:21 (NLT)

We give thanks to the Lord because His faithful love towards us all endures forever!

Epilogue

Before I end, I want to share with you something special that kept me going during our time in France. I tried to pray and read the Bible every day - it didn't always happen, but the more I spent time with Jesus in my 'quiet' place, the more opportunities I gave Him to speak to me. Sometimes I wouldn't hear anything, but when I sensed God speaking to me, I wrote it down in my journal and included the date. My journal was an incredible encouragement to me when I was feeling down, or when we didn't see immediate answers to prayer. I would go back and read it and it would lift my spirit. I encourage you to do the same. When you read something that encourages you, speaks to your heart, or directs you for the day, write it down. You will find it helpful one day when things are perhaps not going as well as you would like them to, and you can look at the verses from the Bible or encouraging quotes and say, "Well, God did speak to me, and I will continue to trust Him." We can be thankful that He has promised to be with us and to bring us to the other side of the storm."

*"Have I not commanded you? Be strong and courageous.
Do not be afraid; do not be discouraged, for the Lord your God
will be with you wherever you go." Joshua 1:9 (NIV)*

Jesus loves you; He wants to have a relationship with you and to give you a life full of joy and purpose. Why do you need Him in your life?

1) You Have a Past

You can't go back, but He can. The Bible says,

> *"Jesus Christ is the same yesterday, today, and forever."*
> *Hebrews 13:8 (NIV)*

He can walk into those places of sin and failure, wipe the slate clean and give you a new beginning.

2) You Need a Friend

Jesus knows the worst about you, yet He believes the best. Why? Because He sees you not as you are, but as you will be when He completes His work in you. What an amazing friend!

3) He Holds the Future

Who else are you going to trust? In His hands you are safe and secure - today, tomorrow and for eternity. His Word says,

> *"For I know the plans I have for you, says the Lord.*
> *They are plans for good and not for evil, to give you a future*
> *and a hope. In those days when you pray, I will listen.*
> *You will find me when you seek me,*
> *if you look for me in earnest."*
> *Jeremiah 29:11-13 (TLB)*

Perhaps you have been inspired by our testimonies and would love to begin a personal relationship with Jesus today. Pray this prayer right now where you are and invite Him to come into your life:

"Dear God, I am sorry for the things that I have done wrong in my life. I ask for Your forgiveness. Thank you for dying on the cross for me to set me free from my sins. Please come into my life and fill me with Your Holy Spirit and be with me forever. Thank You. Amen."

If you have just prayed that prayer, this is the most important decision you will have ever made in your life. Luke 15:10 (NLT) says*: "In the same way, there is joy in the presence of God's angels when even one sinner repents."*

Your next step is to find a church where you can be part of a community of active Bible-believing Christians who can help you in your walk with Jesus. God Bless you!

Beyond Our Limits is a compelling, heart-warming and personal story about a Zimbabwean-born girl who fell in love with a Dutchman. They met in a Christian hostel in Waterloo, London and together felt led to be involved in church planting in Lyon, France. Come with her on an exciting journey of faith where she tackles learning the French language, sharing her faith in a secular society, giving birth in a foreign land, believing for miracles of healing, provision and protection and learning to trust God no matter what life throws at her. *Beyond Our Limits* is jam-packed with adventures and challenges that she will never forget or regret!

Currently, Gaynor van der Hagen leads a Bible study group in her home, loves playing her violin, writing books and travelling. Her whole family are actively involved in a vibrant and fast-growing church. She resides with her husband Paul in Surrey, England. They have four beautiful children and a French Tabby called Leo.

Printed in Great Britain
by Amazon

10143682R00163